P9-DDZ-194

Does Illegal Immigration Harm Society?

Scott Barbour

INCONTROVERSY

San Diego, CA

For more information, contact:
ReferencePoint Press, Inc.
PO Box 27779
San Diego, CA 92198
www. ReferencePointPress.com

Picture credits:
Cover: Istockphoto.com
Maury Aaseng: 12, 23, 71
AP Images: 7, 8, 17, 21, 26, 29, 31, 34, 38, 42, 46, 49, 60, 64, 73, 76, 80
Landov: 19
North Wind: 13, 15

LIBRARY OF CONGRESS CATALOGING-IN-PUBLICATION DATA

Barbour, Scott, 1963-
Does illegal immigration harm society? / by Scott Barbour.
p. cm. — (In controversy)
Includes bibliographical references and index.
ISBN-13: 978-1-60152-085-2
ISBN-10: 1-60152-085-9
1. Illegal aliens—United States. 2. United States—Emigration and immigration—Government policy. I. Title.
JV6483.B37 2009
364.1'370973—dc22

2009009265

Contents

Foreword

In 2008, as the U.S. economy and economies worldwide were falling into one of the worst recessions in modern history, most Americans had difficulty comprehending the complexity, magnitude, and scope of what was happening. As is often the case with a complex, controversial issue such as this historic global economic recession, looking at the problem as a whole can be overwhelming and often does not lead to understanding. One way to better comprehend such a large issue or event is to break it into smaller parts. The intricacies of global economic recession may be difficult to understand, but one can gain insight by instead beginning with an individual contributing factor such as the real estate market. When examined through a narrower lens, complex issues become clearer and easier to evaluate.

This is the idea behind ReferencePoint Press's *In Controversy* series. The series examines the complex, controversial issues of the day by breaking them into smaller pieces. Rather than looking at the stem cell research debate as a whole, a title would examine an important aspect of the debate such as *Is Stem Cell Research Necessary?* or *Is Embryonic Stem Cell Research Ethical?* By studying the central issues of the debate individually, researchers gain a more solid and focused understanding of the topic as a whole.

Each book in the series provides a clear, insightful discussion of the issues, integrating facts and a variety of contrasting opinions for a solid, balanced perspective. Personal accounts and direct quotes from academic and professional experts, advocacy groups, politicians, and others enhance the narrative. Sidebars add depth to the discussion by expanding on important ideas and events. For quick reference, a list of key facts concludes every chapter. Source notes, an annotated organizations list, bibliography, and index provide student researchers with additional tools for papers and class discussion.

The *In Controversy* series also challenges students to think critically about issues, to improve their problem-solving skills, and to sharpen their ability to form educated opinions. As President Barack Obama stated in a March 2009 speech, success in the twenty-first century will not be measurable merely by students' ability to "fill in a bubble on a test but whether they possess 21st century skills like problem-solving and critical thinking and entrepreneurship and creativity." Those who possess these skills will have a strong foundation for whatever lies ahead.

No one can know for certain what sort of world awaits today's students. What we can assume, however, is that those who are inquisitive about a wide range of issues; open-minded to divergent views; aware of bias and opinion; and able to reason, reflect, and reconsider will be best prepared for the future. As the international development organization Oxfam notes, "Today's young people will grow up to be the citizens of the future: but what that future holds for them is uncertain. We can be quite confident, however, that they will be faced with decisions about a wide range of issues on which people have differing, contradictory views. If they are to develop as global citizens all young people should have the opportunity to engage with these controversial issues."

In Controversy helps today's students better prepare for tomorrow. An understanding of the complex issues that drive our world and the ability to think critically about them are essential components of contributing, competing, and succeeding in the twenty-first century.

A Nation of Immigrants—and Laws

On May 12, 2008, agents from U.S. Customs and Immigration Enforcement (ICE), the division of the Department of Homeland Security that enforces the nation's immigration laws, raided Agriprocessors, a kosher meatpacking plant in the small town of Postville, Iowa. In the largest illegal immigrant sweep in the nation's history, officials arrested 389 people on suspicion of identity theft, fraudulent use of social security numbers, and immigration violations. Most of those arrested in the raid were taken to a nearby fairground and informed of their rights and options. Over the next 3 days, the ICE held hearings in which 297 detainees pleaded guilty to various felony charges. Most were sentenced to 5 months in prison, while others received probation; all faced the likelihood of deportation after serving their sentences. In addition to the illegal immigrant employees, 2 of the company's supervisors pleaded guilty to aiding and abetting the harboring of illegal immigrants, and the CEO was indicted on nearly 100 counts of immigration and bank-fraud charges. In November 2008, partly as a result of the raid, Agriprocessors filed for bankruptcy.

Many people criticized the raid, arguing that the immigrants were merely working in order to provide a better life for their families. As stated by John Schlee, a local resident who volunteered to help the families of the arrestees at a local Catholic church: "They're doing work that the American workers don't want to do. They're searching for a better life, and now their families are being torn apart."[1] Indeed, much of the criticism leveled at ICE concerned the fact that many of the workers were parents of young children who found themselves suddenly without a mother or father. In addition, civil libertarians questioned whether the detainees' due process rights were violated by a three-day process in which investigators used scripts to offer plea deals to the immigrants.

"[Illegal immigrants are] doing work that the American workers don't want to do. They're searching for a better life."[1]

— John Schlee, immigrant aid volunteer.

Government officials responded that operations like the Agriprocessors sweep are essential in the fight against illegal immigration. After the raid, Chet Culver, the governor of Iowa, stated: "It is important that we crack down on illegal immigration. Illegal means illegal."[2] Moreover, ICE officials rejected complaints that the arrests were unfair or traumatizing to illegal immigrants and their children. Claude Arnold, special agent in charge of the ICE Office of Investigations in Bloomington, Minnesota, stated: "This operation and its follow up activities were carried out with the utmost professionalism. Dozens of arrested adults were released to care for their children . . . and every detainee was treated with respect and dignity at all times."[3]

Workers leave Agriprocessors meatpacking plant after federal agents raided the plant looking for illegal immigrants. The 2008 raid was the largest illegal immigration sweep in U.S. history.

A Clash of Ideals

The Agriprocessors raid—along with the protests against it—illustrates the competing values that underlie the debate over illegal immigration. America prides itself on being a nation of immigrants. Throughout its history the country has opened its doors to diverse peoples from around the world and invited them to join in the American experiment. They arrived from England, France, and Germany during the colonial era; from Ireland and China in the mid-1800s; from southern and eastern Europe in the late 1800s; and from Southeast Asia in the 1970s. Although rarely welcomed upon their arrival, over time each group became part of America's polyglot society, admired for their tireless pursuit of the American Dream.

After the Agriprocessors raid, Iowa's governor expressed a sentiment shared by others when he said, "Illegal means illegal." This couple makes the same point in a 2009 illegal immigration protest in Texas.

However, in addition to priding themselves on their immigrant history, Americans value another American ideal: the rule of law. Even many people who admire legal immigrants strongly condemn those who would sneak across the border and claim the right to live, work, and enjoy the benefits of American life. Such immigrants, they claim, are harming American society by causing crime, imposing an economic burden on taxpayers, and leaving the nation vulnerable to terrorists. J.D. Hayworth, a representative from Arizona, expresses the view that many people hold toward illegal immigration: "Illegal immigration has a huge impact on crime and prison populations. It is an enormous burden on our health care, education, and welfare systems. It is changing our culture. But the biggest threat comes from the deadly combination of porous borders and weapons of mass destruction finding their way into the hands of terrorist groups."[4] At the very least, critics contend, illegal immigrants are lawbreakers who should be arrested, deported, and forced to the back of the line behind those who patiently wait their turn for permission to enter America legally.

> "It is important that we crack down on illegal immigration. Illegal means illegal."[2]
>
> — Chet Culver, governor of Iowa.

As President Barack Obama has said: "The American people believe that we are a nation of laws—that we have a right and duty to protect our borders. . . . But the American people also know that we are a nation of immigrants."[5] The tension between these two ideals—America as a nation of laws and America as a nation of immigrants—underlies the illegal immigration debate. Some people believe that illegal immigrants are not that different from legal immigrants. Like many of our ancestors, they are industrious people who have left their homeland and traveled hundreds—or even thousands—of miles in search of a better life; the fact that they have crossed the border without permission is of minor consequence. Others acknowledge America's immigrant heritage but insist that the law must be upheld in order to ensure fairness to all and to protect the country from potential harm. In the end, one's perspective on these ideals is likely to color one's views on whether illegal immigration is ultimately harmful or beneficial to American society.

FACTS

- Researchers estimate that of the estimated 11 million illegal immigrants living in the United States, about 7 million are in the workforce.
- In a 2008 Gallup poll, 63 percent of Americans said illegal immigrants cost taxpayers too much, while 31 percent said they pay their fair share of taxes.
- In 2008, U.S. Immigration and Customs Enforcement (ICE) made more than 1,100 criminal arrests during worksite raids for offenses including knowingly hiring illegal aliens, aggravated identity theft, and Social Security fraud.
- ICE agents use various techniques to investigate allegations of workplace immigration violations, including undercover agents, confidential informants, cooperating defendants, and surveillance.

What Are the Origins of the Illegal Immigration Controversy?

Illegal immigration was not an issue in the early years of the United States, because there were few laws controlling the borders. Immigrants were free to come to America's shores and start a new life. Historians describe four waves of immigration, the first being the colonists who settled in New England in the 1600s and 1700s. The second, which arrived between 1820 and 1870, consisted mostly of northern and western Europeans but also included many Chinese. Arriving between 1880 and 1920, the third wave of immigrants hailed mostly from northern and western Europe but also, in smaller numbers, from southern and eastern Europe. During the fourth wave of immigration, beginning in 1965 and continuing to the present, the number of immigrants from Europe has declined while the number of newcomers from Asia and the West Indies has increased. The number of illegal immigrants from Mexico also has risen dramatically, and it is in this era—especially from 1980 to the present—that the issue of illegal immigration has become so controversial.

People Obtaining Lawful Permanent Resident Status and Key Immigration Legislation, 1882–2007

Immigration to the United States has risen and fallen throughout history in response to major events and pieces of legislation.

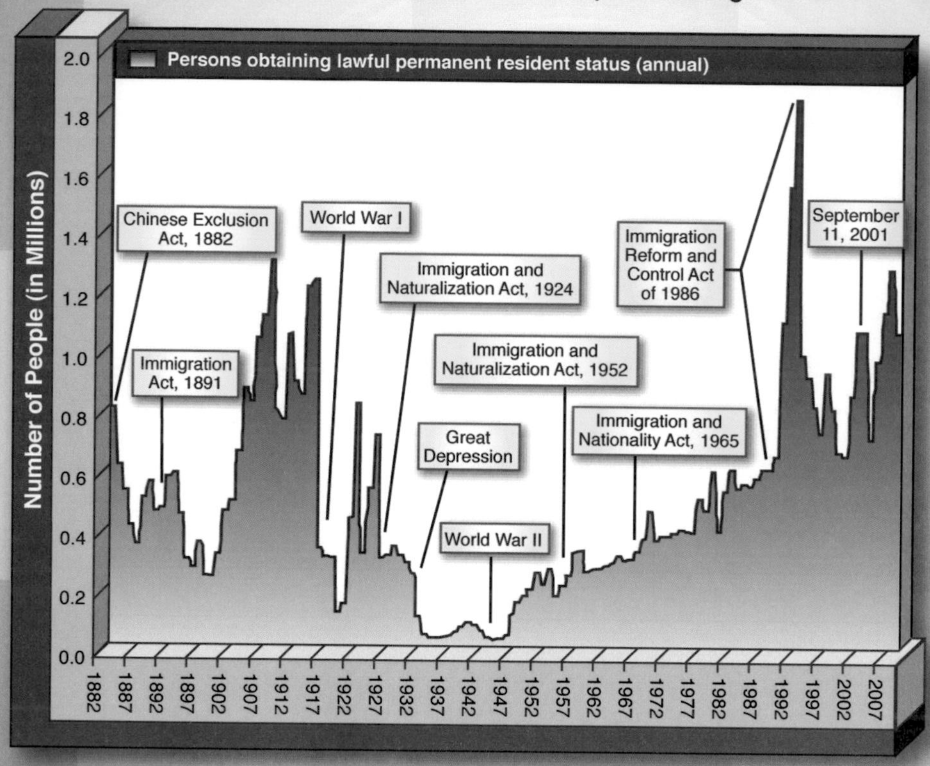

Source: Migration Policy Institute, "Immigrants and the Current Economic Crisis: Research Evidence, Policy Changes, and Implications," January 2009.

Easy Border Crossings

In order to understand the issue of illegal immigration, it is important to know the history of the laws designed to regulate the influx of foreigners. By all accounts the nation's borders were relatively unregulated prior to the twentieth century. However, some controls began to be implemented late in the nineteenth century. In 1875 a law was passed to keep out "undesirables"—specifically, convicts, prostitutes, and Chinese contract laborers. In 1882 that list was expanded to include beggars and the mentally ill. That same year Congress passed the Chinese Exclusion Act, which forbade immigration of nearly all Chinese (not just contract laborers) on the grounds that Chinese immigrants were taking jobs and lowering wages for workers in California. Claire Lui, an editorial assistant at *American Heritage* magazine, argues that the 1882 law created the concept of illegal immigration: "What seemed like fairly minor legislation was the beginning of a major shift in how immigration was perceived in the United States. Now there were two classes of immigrants, legal and illegal."[6] In addition, the Chinese Exclusion Act introduced a policy of controlling immigration on the basis of nationality, a practice that remained in effect until 1965.

Despite passage of the Chinese Exclusion Act and other early laws, America's borders were largely open. As described by Tony Payan, an assistant professor of international relations and foreign policy at the University of Texas at El Paso, few controls existed at the U.S.-Mexico border until the early twentieth century:

> The U.S.-Mexico border was an open border where individuals could cross at will. Even though, strictly speaking, it was illegal to cross between official ports of entry, the United States government had neither the wherewithal nor the desire to guard the border, and bureaucrats on the border were limited to a few at official ports of entry, and no one patrolled the line between them.[7]

Thousands of Chinese laborers helped to build U.S. railways, but Congress decided Chinese contract laborers were "undesirables" in 1875. Another law passed in 1882 effectively blocked Chinese immigration to the United States.

Immigrants, Refugees, and Asylum Seekers

Many different terms are used to describe people who migrate to the United States. An immigrant is a person who moves from one country to another for economic reasons, such as to find a better-paying job, or for personal reasons, such as to reunite with family members. A legal immigrant follows the host country's established procedures for entering and settling in the country. An illegal immigrant enters without permission, sometimes using fraudulent documents, or enters legally with a travel visa and remains in the country after the visa has expired. A refugee is a person who flees his or her home country due to social or political unrest, such as a civil war, or due to political persecution by a repressive government. An asylum seeker is a refugee who enters a foreign country and requests protection. For example, many Cuban Americans in the United States were refugees who fled Fidel Castro's Communist regime and sought asylum in America.

Moreover, the few efforts that were made to control immigration were directed toward the Chinese and others deemed "undesirable." This list did not include Mexicans. Mexicans were considered legitimate immigrants and were allowed to enter freely. Payan continues: "Into the first decade of the 1900s, Mexicans were still allowed to move in and out of the United States unencumbered by any bureaucracies."[8]

Congress Enacts Limits

In the first 2 decades of the twentieth century, large-scale immigration and the outbreak of World War I led to increased distrust of foreigners in America. In response, between 1903 and 1917, Congress passed a series of laws designed to restrict immigration. These laws barred entry to anarchists, "imbeciles," the "feeble-minded," and other disabled people, along with all immigrants from a "barred zone" of countries in the Asia-Pacific region. Although never ratified by Congress, a policy known as the "Gentleman's Agreement" effectively ended immigration from Japan. In addition, all immigrants who were eligible to enter were required to pay an $8 tax and demonstrate literacy in any language.

> "Into the first decade of the 1900s, Mexicans were still allowed to move in and out of the United States unencumbered by any bureaucracies."[7]
>
> — Tony Payan, assistant professor of international relations and foreign policy at the University of Texas at El Paso.

In the 1920s, in response to a continuing influx of foreigners, Congress took several additional steps to control immigration. A 1921 law limited the overall number of immigrants allowed into the country each year. Three years later the Johnson-Reed Act of 1924 set the total number of immigrants from outside the Western Hemisphere at 153,700 per year. The method for determining who would be allowed in was controversial: The white population of the nation was divided by nationality, and proportionate percentages of immigrants from each nationality were permitted entry. This elaborate quota system was designed to reduce the number of immigrants coming from southern and eastern Europe, whom some Americans viewed as inferior or undesirable. Indeed, as stated

Immigrants arrive in New York City in the late 1800s. By the early 1900s, Americans had grown weary of large-scale immigration, and Congress responded by passing new immigration restrictions.

by David M. Reimers, professor emeritus of history at New York University, "The formula ensured that most immigrants would be from such countries as Germany, Ireland, and the United Kingdom."[9]

While the 1924 law did not apply to Mexican immigrants, they too began to feel the effects of the nation's closing borders. As Payan states, "Although Mexicans had been able to move back and forth freely for decades, suddenly . . . they were considered 'foreigners' who did not possess the right to mobility across the boundary."[10] In 1924 Congress also created the Border Patrol to guard the border and prevent people and goods from entering the country illegally. And in 1929 a new law required Mexicans to possess a visa to enter the country. Despite these changes, according to Payan, "people still went back and forth between ports of entry. In fact, up to the 1970s, it was quite easy to cross the border, even illegally."[11]

Tightening and Easing of Border Controls

The middle decades of the twentieth century brought alternating tightening and easing of immigration controls. During World War II, which lasted from 1939 to 1945, the need for foreign workers led to the easing of immigration restrictions. Chinese laborers were once again allowed entry. In addition, the American government created the Bracero Program to import Mexican guest workers. This program permitted legal entry of up to 50,000 agricultural workers and 75,000 railroad workers at any given time. However, due to the need for even more workers, many additional Mexicans immigrated and worked in the country illegally.

"The formula ensured that most immigrants would be from such countries as Germany, Ireland, and the United Kingdom."[9]

— David M. Reimers, professor emeritus of history at New York University.

After the war, the government once again tightened the border. The Bracero Program remained in effect to meet the continuing need for cheap labor. However, in response to anti-immigrant sentiment, in 1954 the government instituted "Operation Wetback" to arrest and deport illegal Mexican immigrants living in the Southwest. More than 1 million were deported, and hundreds of thousands left the country on their own to avoid being captured.

In 1965 immigration laws were changed to reflect the nation's focus on civil rights and racial equality. New legislation did away with quotas based on nationality (which had favored northern Eu-

Mexican migrant workers, employed under the Bracero Program, harvest crops in California in 1964. The Bracero Program supplied farmers with cheap labor. It also gave jobs to thousands of poor, unskilled Mexican laborers.

ropean whites). Instead, the system gave preference first to relatives of American citizens and second to relatives of immigrants already living in the United States. It also favored people with skills that American companies needed. As a result of the 1965 legislation, which set the template for all future immigration policy, a significantly greater number of legal immigrants came from Mexico than any other country from that time until 1976, when the ceiling was set at 20,000 per year.

Government Efforts to Stop Illegal Immigration

Although Mexicans made up the largest proportion of legal immigrants after 1965, many more continued to immigrate illegally. The Bracero Program ended in 1964, but the need for cheap labor did not. Many of the workers who had traveled to the United States legally as guest workers each year began to do so illegally instead. Indeed, their numbers swelled as rapid industrialization

A Human Story

The issue of illegal immigration is often about numbers—the number of illegal immigrants who enter the country each year, the number apprehended at the border, the number who live illegally in the country. However, behind each number is a human being with a particular story. The American Friends Services Committee, a Quaker organization that advocates the humane treatment of illegal immigrants, tells one story:

> Luis had lived and worked in the U.S. for ten years. His wife and their three children lived with him. Early in 2008, Luis was pulled over for a routine traffic stop by Phoenix police. Having no driver's license, Luis was turned over to Immigration and Customs Enforcement. Because he refused to sign voluntary deportation papers, he sat in jail for six months before being deported in August. On September 15, Luis was found dead in the Arizona border desert. Trying to get back to his wife, his seven year old, his four year old, and the three month old baby daughter he had never met, he died of dehydration and exposure.

Although Americans may disagree about the policy issues surrounding illegal immigration, few would deny the tragedy of stories such as this one.

American Friends Services Committee, *A New Path Toward Humane Immigration Policy*, February 2009, p. 13. www.afsc.org.

in Mexico left many farm laborers unable to find jobs in Mexico. In addition, while Mexicans were still the biggest cohort of legal immigrants, the overall number of those permitted in each year was reduced to 20,000 in 1976, a mere fraction of the number seeking entry. As a result of these and other factors, illegal immigration from Mexico became a major issue in the late 1970s and early 1980s. By 1986 it was estimated that 4 million to 5 million illegal Mexican immigrants were living in the United States. This marks the beginning of the illegal immigration issue as it is known today—an issue that primarily focuses on illegal immigrants from Mexico and Central America.

In response to growing concerns about illegal immigration, Congress passed the Immigration Reform and Control Act of 1986 (IRCA). The law had two facets. First, it offered amnesty (that is, it granted legal status) to illegal immigrants living in the United

Construction crews in Arizona weld sheet metal into place as part of construction of a fence that separates the United States and Mexico. In 1996, Congress ordered construction of a fence along the busiest sections of the border. Work on the fence is ongoing.

States who met certain conditions. Second, it imposed penalties, or sanctions, on employers who knowingly hired illegal immigrant workers. Most commentators agree that the law was unsuccessful. About 3 million illegal immigrants applied for amnesty, but countless others simply remained in the country illegally. In addition, the employer sanction requirements proved easy to evade and went largely unenforced. Consequently, the law did little to deter people from crossing the border illegally. As stated by Katherine Fennelly, a professor of public affairs at the University of Minnesota, "Few employers were actually sanctioned, and unauthorized immigrants continued to enter the U.S."[12]

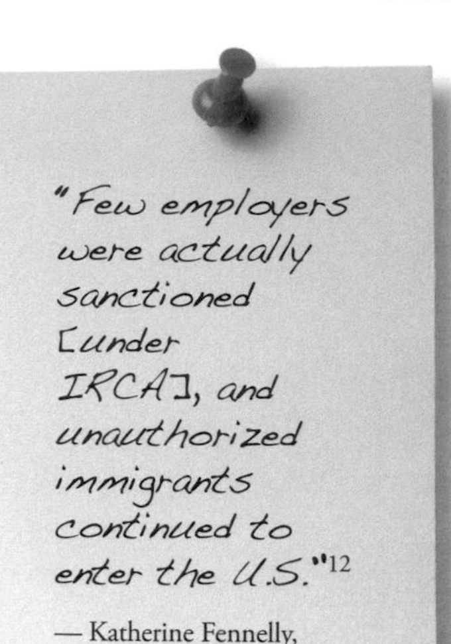

In response to the perceived failure of IRCA, in 1996 Congress passed the Illegal Immigration Reform and Immigrant Responsibility Act (IIRIRA). The law made it easier to deport illegal immigrants and immigrant felons, increased the number of Border Patrol agents by 1,000 per year over 5 years, and mandated the construction of a fence along the busiest sections of the border. As a result, the number of Border Patrol agents rose from over 6,000 in 1996 to over 11,000 in 2002. Formidable fences were erected, and new vehicles and sophisticated surveillance tools were put to use.

Holding the Line Against Illegal Immigration

With its beefed up personnel and other resources, the Border Patrol instituted several military-like operations in the 1990s: Operation Hold the Line in El Paso, Texas; Operation Safeguard in Arizona; and Operation Gatekeeper in California. These efforts focused on areas of the border with heavy illegal traffic. They succeeded in slowing immigration in those areas. However, in some cases the immigration routes simply changed, often taking border crossers through mountain and desert regions in which their lives were at risk. As a result, the number of immigrants dying while trying to cross the border increased dramatically. The Government Accountability Office (GAO) reports that the number of bodies found along the U.S.-Mexico border doubled between 1995 and 2005, with most of the increase occurring in the Arizona desert.

Nearly 3,000 bodies of illegal immigrants were recovered along the border between 1995 and 2004, an average of 300 per year.

Despite the government's efforts with IRCA, IIRIRA, and border enforcement, illegal immigration continued at a steady pace throughout the 1990s and into the first years of the twenty-first century. The Department of Homeland Security estimates that 3.5 million illegal immigrants lived in the United States in 1990. By 2000 that number had doubled to 7 million, an increase of 350,000 per year on average. Throughout these years more than half of the illegal immigrants living in the United States came from Mexico, with many others from El Salvador, Guatemala, and other Central American countries. Other major sources of illegal immigrants included China, the Dominican Republic, and Haiti.

As illegal immigrants continued to arrive in the 1990s, many Americans became frustrated by the government's failure to address the problem. States with large populations of illegal immigrants, such as Arizona, California, and Texas, began to feel the burden as immigrants competed for jobs and relied on social services during a time of economic recession. Politicians and citizens alike began to protest the federal government's inadequate response. One notable example occurred in 1994 in California, where voters approved Proposition 187, a state initiative that prevented illegal immigrants

During Operation Gatekeeper, a U.S. Border Patrol agent escorts illegal immigrants across a stretch of California desert after a Border Patrol helicopter spotted the group hiding in low-lying brush.

from receiving certain social services, including public education and nonemergency health care. Most provisions of the proposition were later declared unconstitutional by a U.S. district court.

Writing in *Salon,* editor and journalist Anthony York stated that "Proposition 187 was the beginning of the anti-immigrant brush fire that spread across the country."[13] Indeed, following the bill's passage, similar legislation was introduced in other states. For example, Arizona passed and enacted Proposition 200, which requires proof of citizenship to register to vote or to apply for public benefits.

Immigration Control in the Post-9/11 Era

The September 11, 2001, terrorist attacks on America cast a new spotlight on illegal immigration. The 19 hijackers who carried out the attacks had entered the country legally using student visas. However, 4 of the hijackers' visas had expired at the time of the attack. People who stay in the country after their visas expire are considered illegal immigrants. As a result of the security breach, border enforcement came to be seen as not merely a law enforcement problem but a national security issue. In response, the Immigration and Naturalization Service, the government agency that had been responsible for overseeing the nation's immigration policy, was replaced by U.S. Immigration and Customs Enforcement under the aegis of the newly created Department of Homeland Security. More money and resources were allocated for border enforcement: By 2009 the Border Patrol had more than 17,000 agents and a budget of $8.8 billion.

In addition to beefing up enforcement, the government again tried to address the problem of illegal immigration via legislation. In 2006 President George W. Bush pushed for a bill that would have tightened employer sanctions and provided a path to legalization for illegal immigrants living in the United States. After intense debate each house of Congress passed a version of the legislation but failed to reconcile their bills into one they could all agree on. A chief point of contention was the legalization component; many conservatives characterized it as a form of amnesty and opposed the bill because of that.

Illegal Immigration Today

Although the bill sought by President Bush did not pass, illegal immigration appears to have slowed since 2006. A study by the Pew Hispanic Center, a public policy research organization specializing in issues that affect Hispanics, found that the number of illegal immigrants entering the country each year declined from 800,000 between 2000 and 2004 to 500,000 between 2005 and 2008. Illegal immigrant apprehensions by the Department of Homeland Security are down as well, from almost 1.3 million in 2005 to fewer than 1 million in 2007. The number of illegal immigrants residing in the United States also appears to have declined, although estimates vary among agencies and institutions. The Pew Center reports a drop from 12.4 million in 2007 to 11.9 million in 2008, while the conservative Center for Immigration Studies reports a drop from 12.5 million in 2007 to 11.2 million

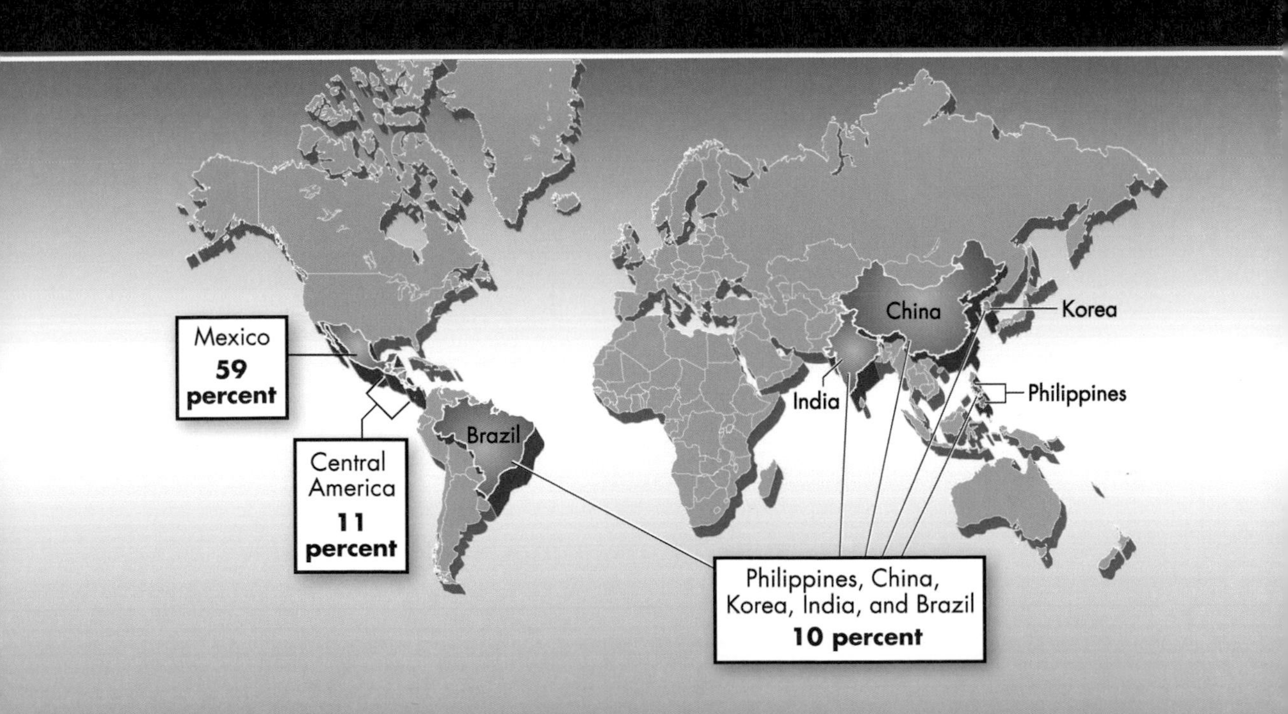

Source: 2005 Core Knowledge® National Conference, Coming to America: U.S. Immigration, 6th Grade.

in 2008. The Migration Policy Institute, a nonpartisan think tank devoted to the study of immigration, theorizes that the causes of the slowdown in illegal immigration may include a sharp downturn in the U.S. economy and increased enforcement of immigration policies.

The current illegal immigrant population is made up mostly of immigrants from Mexico (59 percent) and Central America (at least 11 percent). However, it also includes hundreds of thousands of people from other nations around the world. Migrants from the Philippines, China, Korea, India, and Brazil constitute 10 percent of the undocumented immigrant population, at about 2 percent each. Most of these illegal immigrants sneak across the border or use fake documents to enter through official ports of entry. Many others enter legally with travel visas and remain in the country after their visas have expired. Experts estimate that as many as 40 percent (over 4 million) of the nation's approximately 11 million illegal immigrants entered in this way. Still others attempt to reach U.S. shores by boat, most notably Haitians and Cubans bound for Florida (although Cubans, once on U.S. shores, are eligible for legal status).

Many of the illegal immigrants who come to America are aided by human smugglers who make huge profits while placing immigrants at great risk. Mexican smugglers called "coyotes" often lead migrants through desert terrain and abandon them when they succumb to harsh conditions. Chinese smugglers called "snake-heads" charge as much as $60,000 to $80,000 to sneak immigrants into the country. Chinese immigrants typically travel legally to Bangkok, then use fake IDs to continue on various routes before entering the United States via Mexico. Often they rely on coyotes to make the final border crossing. In some instances Chinese immigrants are flown or trucked across the border. For example, in September 2008, 23 Chinese nationals were among 50 illegal immigrants found packed in an 18-wheeler at a southern Texas checkpoint. In 2007 over 1,600 Chinese were apprehended attempting to enter the United States illegally.

A Nation Divided on Immigration

With people from all parts of the globe clamoring to enter the United States, illegal immigration remains an extremely divisive issue in American society. Most people agree that laws against illegal immigration should be enforced and that people who want to come to America should do so through the legal process. However, many people are quick to point out that the legal process is cumbersome and not available to many who simply want to come to America to work. Moreover, opinions differ on how illegal immigrants should be treated once they have arrived in the country. Some view illegal immigrants as invaders seeking to commit crimes, abuse social services, or at best, steal jobs from U.S. workers. These critics call for punitive measures such as deportation. Others defend illegal immigrants as admirable, hardworking, brave souls who are simply doing what immigrants of previous generations have done: pursuing the American Dream. Those who hold this view are more likely to favor a more lenient approach, including some form of legalization.

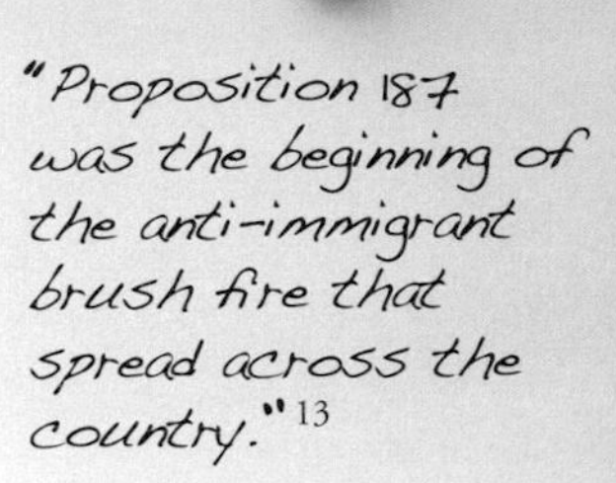

In political terms the issue of illegal immigration is extremely complex. Cultural conservatives tend to be the harshest critics of illegal immigrants, viewing them as a threat to the traditional American values, culture, and way of life because they are unlikely to assimilate into society by learning the language and customs. They are also most likely to emphasize the crime and security risks posed by such newcomers. On the other hand, economic conservatives—that is, free-market capitalists—are traditionally much more sympathetic toward illegal immigrants, seeing them as a source of cheap labor and an overall boon to society due to their industriousness and their will to succeed.

Political liberals are no less divided on the issue of illegal immigration. Labor leaders argue that illegal immigrants threaten U.S. workers by taking jobs and driving down wages. Many African Americans are also critics of illegal immigration because many of them compete with immigrants for jobs. In addition, because many blacks live in the low-income neighborhoods where illegal immigrants settle, they are more likely to feel the brunt of criminal activity committed by such immigrants, including gang violence. Environmentalists, who tend to be characterized as liberals, also view illegal immigration as a negative because they believe that people who enter the country illegally contribute to overpopulation, thereby threatening the environment. On the other hand many white liberals sympathize with illegal immigrants on humanitarian grounds. They point out that most illegal immigrants have left regions of extreme poverty and are simply seeking a better life for themselves or hoping to earn money to send home to their families. Some liberal religious groups, most notably Catholics and Quakers, have made the humane treatment of immigrants—whether legal or illegal—a central goal of their mission.

These various conservative and liberal views on immigration are, of course, generalizations. There are exceptions to every position—for example, blacks who defend illegal immigrants and white liberals who oppose them. However, the fact remains that opinions on the issue are varied, complex, and entrenched. Advocacy groups have sprung up on both sides of the issue, often attacking one another with charges, or at least implied accusations, of racism. Political pundits and media personalities debate the issue,

U.S. Coast Guard personnel stand guard over Chinese immigrants who had hoped to enter the United States illegally. Several hundred immigrants pack the vessel's hold as they await processing and likely deportation.

while politicians favor one side or the other depending on their ideology, their constituency, or the audience at hand. In the end each person's opinion on the issue will likely depend on a mixture of his or her experience, political orientation, and personal values and beliefs.

FACTS

- **The Chinese immigrants who helped build the railroads in the nineteenth century were referred to as "coolies." This term is now considered a racial slur.**

- **The word *wetback* is an extremely offensive derogatory term for an illegal immigrant. It originated in reference to immigrants crossing the Rio Grande River, presumably getting their backs wet in the process.**

- **U.S. president Ronald Reagan, one of the most revered free-market conservatives in the nation's history, was a staunch supporter of both legal and illegal immigrants.**

- **Men between the ages of 25 and 34 make up the largest gender/age category of illegal immigrants living in the United States, at 2.5 million.**

- **In a 2007 *New York Times*/CBS poll, 61 percent of Americans said illegal immigration is a very serious problem, 30 percent said it is somewhat serious, and 6 percent said it is not too serious.**

CHAPTER TWO

Does Illegal Immigration Harm the American Economy?

Most illegal immigrants come to America to find work that pays more than they can make in their home countries. Whether they come from Mexico, Guatemala, or China, immigrants typically risk the hazards of crossing the border illegally mainly because they seek to escape poverty in their homelands. As stated by Ramesh Ponnuru, a senior editor for *National Review* magazine, "Illegal immigrants come here for the same reasons legal immigrants do: chiefly, to make a better life for themselves and their families."[14]

Experts estimate that 7 million of the approximately 11 million illegal immigrants in the United States hold jobs of some sort, often as unskilled laborers. Though pay for these jobs is low by American standards, it represents a significant amount of money for workers from poor countries. Mexican author Mario Vargas Llosa explains that illegal immigrants:

> [Take] jobs that US citizens don't want to do. They are cleaners, minders for old people, night watchmen, lettuce pickers under the burning sun, or working in factories and

shops—low-level, precarious jobs. Only they are prepared to do these jobs which, for the standard of living of the country, are poorly paid. But not from their point of view: for these immigrant workers, the low wages are a fortune.[15]

As Vargas Llosa suggests, many people view the presence of illegal immigrants as mutually beneficial for both the immigrants, who make higher wages in America than at home, and U.S. citizens, who rely on the cheap labor. While some critics argue that illegal immigrants harm low-skill American workers by competing for jobs and accepting lower pay, immigrant supporters insist that such claims are exaggerated. As stated by David Card, an economist at the University of California at Berkeley, "Evidence that immigrants have harmed the opportunities of less-educated natives is scant."[16]

In addition to benefiting immigrants and employers, illegal immigration is also believed to be essential to the American economy. The jobs illegal immigrants do are crucial. And some experts contend that it is equally critical that these jobs be done for low

The sun beats down on migrant workers who are picking lettuce on a Southern California farm. Lettuce picking and other similar jobs pay little but the wages represent a fortune to unskilled workers from poor countries.

wages. For example, according to Llewellyn D. Howell, professor of international management at Thunderbird School of Global Management and president of Howell International, a consulting company, low wages are especially important in order to keep America's agricultural sector vital and competitive. Howell states:

> A part of agricultural competitiveness is that, where mechanization is not possible—picking low-lying fruit and vegetables, food processing, tree and vine trimming—manual labor is necessary. Costs, however, still have to be kept as low as possible to compete in a globalized economy. New immigrants (for the most part illegals) are taking these jobs at these wages and keeping the U.S. economy afloat.[17]

Howell and others suggest that a continued supply of illegal immigrants is essential to maintain the success of America's economy—especially in agriculture and other industries that rely on unskilled labor.

Removing illegal immigrants from the workforce would have a devastating effect on the nation's financial health, some experts predict. Without the pool of illegal immigrant labor, employers would be forced to comply with laws regulating the workplace. As a result, they would have to pay higher wages. To pay these higher wages, they would have to eliminate jobs and raise their prices for products. The rise in prices would lead to less spending by consumers, which in turn would cause businesses to fail and more jobs to be lost. Thus, it is the very illegality of illegal immigrants that makes them essential.

Driving Down Wages

Not everyone agrees that illegal immigration is necessary or good for the American economy. In fact, some critics insist that illegal immigrants harm the economy by, among other things, driving down wages. Because illegal immigrants are willing to work for low wages, the argument goes, American workers are forced to accept lower pay when competing for the same jobs. Not surprisingly, it is the less-educated citizens who are the most adversely affected. As stated by Steven A. Camarota, the director of research at the Center

A farm worker unloads eggplants in Florida. Some crops can be harvested by machines while others have to be done by hand. Many illegal immigrants are drawn to the United States for these types of jobs.

for Immigration Studies (CIS), a public policy research organization that advocates restrictions on both legal and illegal immigration: "Common sense, economic theory, and a fair reading of the research on this question indicate that allowing in so many immigrants (legal and illegal) with relatively little education reduces the job prospects for Americans with little education. These are the Americans who are already the poorest workers." Camarota goes on to say that African American workers have been harmed the most by illegal immigration, noting that "immigration accounted for about a third of the decline in the employment rate of the least-educated African American men over the last few decades."[18]

Research supports the claim that illegal immigration drives down wages, especially for the least-educated workers. Harvard economics professors George Borjas and Lawrence Katz studied the impact of immigration from 1980 to 2000. They concluded that as a result of the influx of immigrants from Mexico, the wages of average American workers fell 3 percent and the wages of American workers who were high school dropouts fell 8 percent.

Taking Jobs Americans Want

The commonly held view that illegal immigrants do the jobs that Americans do not want is not universally accepted. Some experts say that Americans would gladly take those jobs if the wages were not driven down by competition from illegal immigrants. As stated by writer Thomas R. Eddlem: "These are jobs that Americans 'do not want' only because illegal immigrants have depressed the wage scale for the positions. Take away the illegal immigrants, and the market would raise wages to the level where Americans would take the jobs."[19]

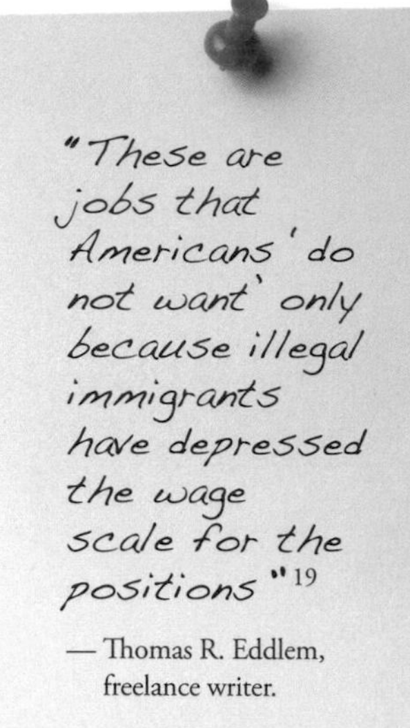

Anecdotal evidence seems to confirm the argument that American workers would take low-skilled jobs if competition from illegal immigrants were removed. In 2006 federal officials raided a Crider Poultry plant in Stillmore, Georgia, and removed 120 illegal immigrant workers. As a result, the company raised its wages and began to hire American citizens, including local homeless men, probationers, and poor African Americans. As reported in the *Wall Street Journal*, "For the first time since significant numbers of Latinos began arriving in Stillmore in the late 1990s, the plant's processing lines were made up predominately of African Americans."[20]

Taxes and Social Services

In addition to the debate over the impact of illegal immigration on jobs and wages, there is also debate over whether illegal immigrants pay their fair share of taxes. Of special concern is whether the taxes paid by illegal immigrants cover the costs they place on governments (federal, state, and local) in the form of health care, education, incarceration, welfare, and other social services.

Calculating the cost-benefit ratio of illegal immigration is difficult for various reasons. For starters, illegal immigrants are not tracked, so researchers must estimate not only how many illegal immigrants there are, but how much they pay in taxes and how much they rely on government services. In order to make these estimates, researchers must make certain assumptions, which in turn can have a large impact on the outcome of their studies. Jeffrey Passal, a senior research specialist at the Pew Hispanic Center, a public policy research organization, describes the challenges of researching the costs of illegal immigration:

The problem with cost studies that assess budget impacts from illegal immigrants to federal and state governments and the economy is that the results you get depend a lot on the assumptions that you make. . . . For example: . . . Are children included as part of the costs of undocumented immigrants? What factors are included as part of general government costs? There is no universal agreement on these and many other questions that various people use to calculate the costs related to illegal immigration.[21]

The Legacy of *Plyler v. Doe*

In its 1982 decision in *Plyler v. Doe*, the U.S. Supreme Court ruled that it was unconstitutional to deny a public education to illegal immigrant children. The case involved four families from the town of Tyler, Texas, who sought to overturn a state law that allowed schools to bar illegal immigrants. The Court found that the law was unconstitutional because it violated the immigrants' right to equal protection as guaranteed by the Fourteenth Amendment. One of the arguments in favor of the law was that children of illegal immigrants were unlikely to remain in the country and participate in U.S. society; therefore, the costs of educating them would not lead to benefits for the nation. In his majority opinion Justice William J. Brennan rejected this argument, stating that "many of the undocumented children . . . will remain in this country indefinitely, and . . . some will become lawful residents or citizens of the United States." Twenty-five years later, three of the original four families still lived in Tyler. One couple had 16 grandchildren, all of whom were integrated into Tyler's school community, engaged in such activities as basketball, choir, soccer, and cheerleading.

William J. Brennan, "U.S. Supreme Court: *Plyler v. Doe,* 457 U.S. 202 (1982)," FindLaw. http://caselaw.lp.findlaw.com.

In short, researching the economic cost-benefit ratio of illegal immigration is an inexact science at best.

Income Tax, Social Security, and Welfare

The question of how much illegal immigrants pay in income tax and Social Security payments provides a good example of how hard it is to measure the economic costs and benefits of illegal immigration. Some illegal immigrants are paid "under the table"—that is, their employers skirt the laws and pay them in cash, without deducting Social Security or income tax withholdings. Thus, these illegal immigrants pay no Social Security or income tax. On the other hand, the laws now allow illegal immigrants to report earnings to the Internal Revenue Service even though they do not have a Social Security number. Therefore, many illegal immigrants report their income and pay taxes. In addition, these immigrants contribute to the Social Security fund but never receive Social Security benefits. Moreover, just like citizens, illegal immigrants pay sales taxes and property taxes (directly, as property owners, and

After a 2006 immigration raid on Crider Poultry in Georgia, the company raised its wages and hired American citizens. This newly hired employee works on the canning line, a job previously done by illegal immigrant workers.

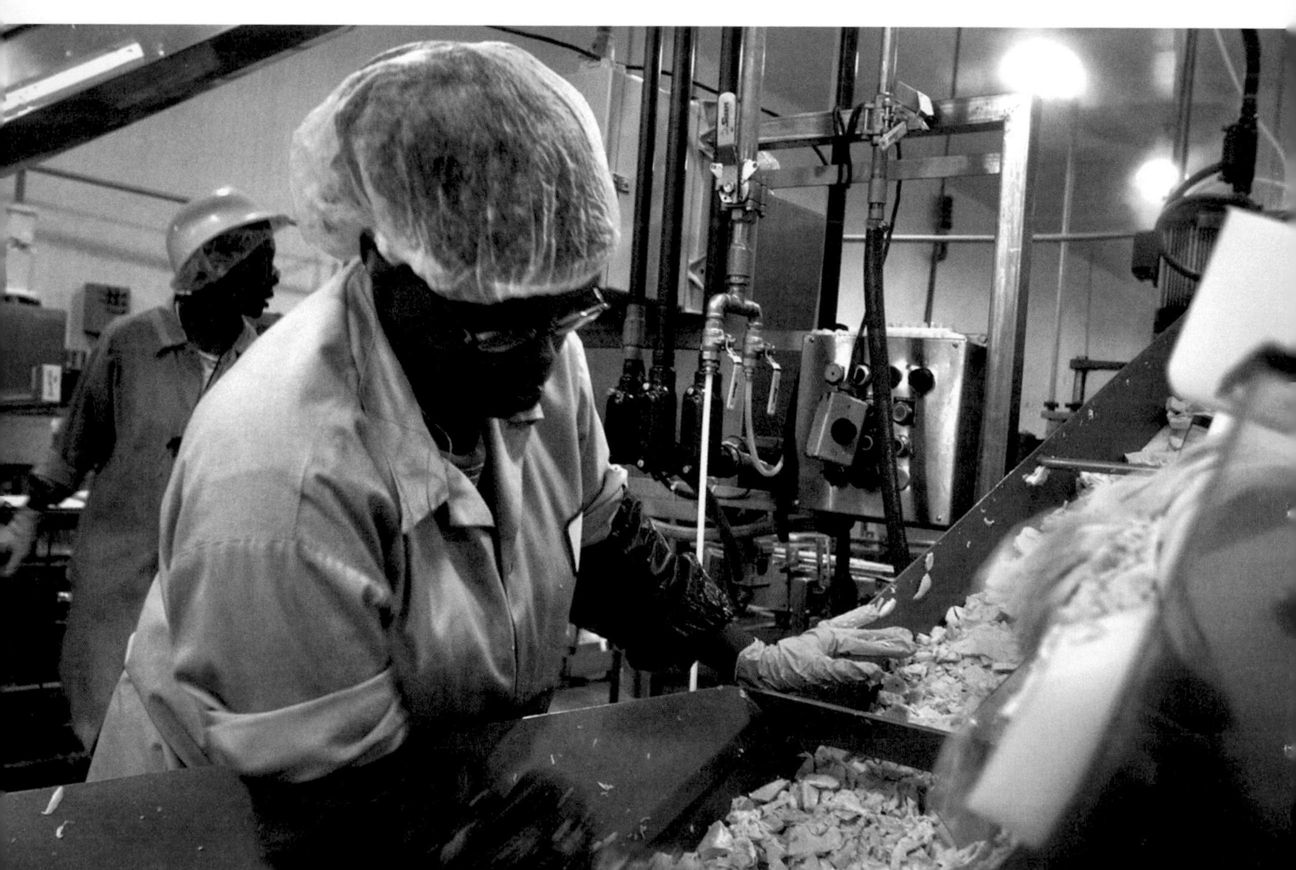

indirectly, as renters). Ferreting out all these variables is a daunting task for researchers.

Welfare provides another example of the difficulty in measuring the economic costs and benefits of illegal immigration. Many people assume that illegal immigrants come to America seeking welfare benefits. However, illegal immigrants are not entitled to these benefits. While some likely obtain benefits using forged documents, research indicates that these numbers are low. Complicating the issue is the 14th Amendment to the U.S. Constitution, which states that any person born on U.S. soil is an American citizen. Thus, the American-born children of illegal immigrants are U.S. citizens and are entitled to benefits even while their parents are ineligible. Again, the assumptions researchers make about these variables can have a profound effect on the outcomes of their studies.

"Allowing in so many immigrants (legal and illegal) with relatively little education reduces the job prospects for Americans with little education."[22]

— Steven A. Camarota, director of research at the Center for Immigration Studies.

The Costs of Illegal Immigration

Despite these challenges many studies have been done in recent decades. Some have lumped legal and illegal immigration together and have reached different conclusions about the tax-benefit ratio, with some finding an overall economic benefit and others finding a deficit. However, most studies that have focused specifically on illegal immigration have found that illegal immigrants cost the government more in public services—especially education and health care—than they pay in taxes.

The CIS examined the costs of illegal immigration to the federal government and concluded that costs outweighed tax payments. In 2002, according to the CIS, illegal immigrants imposed $26.3 billion in costs on the federal government but paid only $16 billion in taxes, resulting in a net deficit of almost $10.4 billion. The largest costs were for Medicaid ($2.2 billion), food assistance programs ($1.9 billion), the federal prison and court system ($1.6 billion), and federal aid to schools ($1.4 billion). The CIS noted that the disparity was not the result of massive use of services by illegal immigrants but by their very low tax contributions: "On average, the costs that illegal households impose on federal coffers are less than half [those] of other households, but their tax payments are only one-fourth [those] of other households."[22]

Economic Burden on State and Local Governments

Other studies have focused on the costs illegal immigration imposes on state and local governments. The impact of illegal immigration on state and local governments is especially controversial: Controlling immigration is the responsibility of the federal government. However, the federal government's failure to stem the influx of illegal immigrants ends up burdening state and local governments, which shoulder the economic costs for providing services such as education and emergency health care. Moreover, the federal government typically does not sufficiently reimburse state and local governments for these costs.

The federal government's failure to compensate state and local governments for the costs of supplying services to illegal immigrants strikes critics as especially unfair. Not only does the federal government fail to stop immigrants from entering the country illegally and burdening the state and local governments, it forbids these smaller governments from withholding certain services from illegal immigrants. For example, in its 1982 decision *Plyler v. Doe*, the U.S. Supreme Court declared it unconstitutional to bar illegal immigrant children from schools. Thus, the federal government essentially requires school districts to educate illegal immigrants in the public schools without providing them with the financial resources they need to do so.

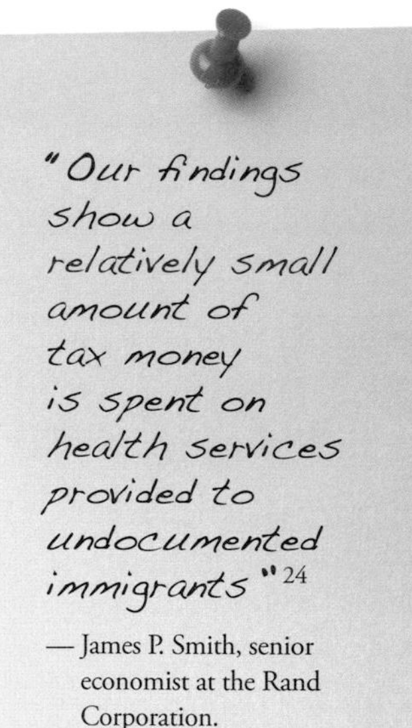

—James P. Smith, senior economist at the Rand Corporation.

In addition, states and localities are required to treat illegal immigrants in hospital emergency rooms—again, with little or no federal economic assistance. Compounding this problem is the fact that most illegal immigrants lack medical insurance and are therefore more likely to use the emergency room for routine medical needs, ratcheting up the costs of health care even more.

A recent study by the Congressional Budget Office (CBO) confirmed that state and local governments shoulder an economic burden for supplying services to illegal immigrants. The CBO reviewed 29 studies that evaluated the impact of illegal immigration on the budgets of state and local governments. The CBO conclud-

An American Success Story

While most illegal immigrants come to America to work in low-skill jobs, some achieve greater levels of success, and some even start their own businesses. Jorge Fierro provides one example. Crossing the U.S.-Mexico border illegally in 1985, Fierro went first to Wyoming and then to Utah, where he studied English and worked as a dishwasher. Soon after arriving in America, he bought a can of refried beans and was so disappointed by the quality that he decided to start his own business selling authentic Mexican-style beans. In 1997, having gained legal status by marrying a U.S. citizen, Fierro began preparing and selling beans at the Salt Lake City Farmers Market. One year later, with the help of a $10,000 loan, he opened a small market of his own. By 2008 Fierro's company, Rico, offered more than 150 products, including chili verde, mango salsa, pico de gallo, tamales, and tortillas, with distribution to nearly 60 supermarkets in Utah and Nevada. Also in 2008, Fierro opened a restaurant, Café by Rico, in Salt Lake City.

ed that the taxes paid by illegal immigrants to state and local governments did not cover the costs of the services the governments provided. In addition, while the state and local governments did receive federal aid to help cover the costs incurred by illegal immigrants, the aid was not enough to cover the expenses fully.

A study focused specifically on California provides further evidence that illegal immigration is a burden on states. The Federation for American Immigration Reform (FAIR), an advocacy organization that supports greater restrictions on immigration, studied the state costs for education, medical care, and incarceration of illegal immigrants. The researchers concluded that the state spent $10.5 billion on these costs: $7.7 billion for education, $1.4 billion for medical care, and $1.4 billion for incarceration. However, the state only received $1.7 billion in taxes from illegal immigrants, leaving a loss of $8.8 billion. FAIR insists that its study does not measure the full magnitude of the burden illegal immigrants place on California: "The total costs of illegal immigration to the state's taxpayers would be considerably higher if other cost areas such as special English instruction, school feeding programs, or welfare benefits for American workers displaced by illegal alien workers were added into the equation.[23]

Although researchers tend to agree that illegal immigrants are a net economic burden on society, they disagree over the extent of the costs illegal immigrants generate. For example, the CIS study on the costs of illegal immigration found that the federal government spends $2.5 billion a year in Medicaid payments for illegal immigrants. However, a study by the Rand Corporation, a think tank based in Santa Monica, California, found that state and local governments combined spend only $1.1 billion on health care for illegal immigrants, a considerably lower amount. James P. Smith, a senior economist at Rand and one of the authors of the study, states, "Our findings show a relatively small amount of tax

Hospital emergency rooms across the country often have long waits. Most illegal immigrants lack medical insurance, which forces them to go to emergency rooms for routine medical needs.

money is spent on health services provided to undocumented immigrants."[24] Dana Goldman, a coauthor of the study, suggests that illegal immigrants use fewer health services because they are less likely to have health insurance and are "generally healthier than the native-born population."[25]

Profiting from Illegality

Despite all the debates over the economic costs and benefits of illegal immigrants, one fact remains: Illegal immigrants live and work in America, and more continue to arrive every day. Why is this situation allowed to continue? It seems obvious that if illegal immigration posed a major threat to the economic survival of the nation, the government would make more of an effort to stem the influx of immigrants and prevent them from working in America. The fact that millions of illegal immigrants are permitted to live and work in the United States seems proof that they provide some benefit.

"By filling the unskilled-labor gap illegal immigrants contribute to keeping the U.S. economy productive, competitive and prosperous."[26]

— Ernesto Zedillo, former president of Mexico.

The answer to this riddle most likely lies in the theories of pro-immigrant economists. Free-market economists insist that immigrant labor—both skilled and unskilled—is crucial to the economy. Illegal immigration fills the need for unskilled workers by supplying a large pool of laborers at the lowest possible costs. These immigrants may impose some economic costs on government, but perhaps these costs are a reasonable trade-off for illegal immigrants' contribution to keeping business vital and the gross domestic product growing. In short, illegal immigrant labor is desirable *because* it is illegal and therefore cheap enough to meet the needs of the U.S. economy. As explained by former Mexican president Ernesto Zedillo:

> Without [illegal immigrant] workers, productivity and economic growth would be slower; there would be fewer jobs for skilled labor; Americans' earnings would be reduced; and some service sectors now thriving would become stagnant, while others would be at risk of collapsing. In short, by filling the unskilled-labor gap illegal immigrants contribute to keeping the U.S. economy productive, competitive and prosperous.[26]

It may be too cynical to say that the American government is intentionally sustaining the illegal status of a large segment of the population in order to fulfill the needs of a free-market economy. However, there is no doubt than many employers and industries profit from the continued presence of illegal immigrants in the labor force.

FACTS

- **A 2006 study by the Texas State Comptroller found that illegal immigrants created $1.58 billion in state revenue and cost $1.16 billion in state services.**

- **According to the Urban Institute, illegal immigrants make up 4 percent of the overall population, but they constitute 23 percent of the lower-skilled labor force.**

- **A 2008 Gallup poll found that 79 percent of Americans believe illegal immigrants take low-skill jobs that Americans do not want; only 15 percent believe illegal immigrants take jobs Americans want.**

- **In a 2008 Gallup poll, 71 percent of whites and 62 percent of blacks—but only 30 percent of Hispanics—said that illegal immigrants cost taxpayers too much money.**

- **According to the 2005 *Economic Report of the President*, 50 percent of illegal immigrant workers contribute to the Social Security fund.**

Does Illegal Immigration Harm American Culture?

In April and May of 2006, hundreds of thousands of pro-immigrant demonstrators took to the streets in cities nationwide. Many of the marchers were illegal immigrants who brazenly chanted and carried signs alongside citizens and legal immigrants. They marched to oppose proposed federal legislation that would have increased the penalties for illegal immigration and classified illegal immigrants, along with people who aided them, as felons. More generally, they advocated increased immigrants' rights and amnesty for illegal immigrants. Jaime Contreras, president of the National Capital Immigration Coalition, one of the groups involved in organizing the demonstrations, explained the purpose of the protests: "What we want to achieve is to send a very strong message to the Senate, to the Congress . . ., that we are tired, that we work very hard. . . . We come to this country not to take from America, but to make America strong. And we do not deserve to be treated the way we have been treated."[27]

In the first demonstrations, held on April 10, many marchers carried Mexican flags, images of revolutionary Che Guevara, and signs advocating *reconquista*, Mexico's reconquering of California and other parts of the Southwest. These symbols left many Americans wondering if the latest wave of immigrants—especially illegal immigrants from Mexico—have any real interest in assimilating

Demonstrators in Philadelphia wave the flag and colors of Mexico during a 2006 immigrant rights march. Scenes like this caused many Americans to wonder if recent immigrants—legal and illegal—really want to be part of American society.

into American culture or if they are just here to make some money. This concern was summed up by Dan Stein, the executive director of the Federation for American Immigration Reform (FAIR), a group that opposes large-scale immigration and favors tough enforcement of immigration laws:

> The illegal alien protests . . . provided evidence of the deep social divisions in American society. . . . America is clearly failing to assimilate large numbers of immigrants into the mainstream of society. Millions of people who are living in this country do not identify with this nation and see it as nothing more than a place where they can earn more money and receive better social services than in their homelands.[28]

In response to such criticism, protesters at subsequent demonstrations carried American and Mexican flags in roughly equal numbers. But critics were not convinced of the sincerity of this gesture, believing that the protesters were simply pretending to identify with America in order to win over public support.

Melting Pot or Tossed Salad?

The 2006 protests—and the backlash they created—highlighted a central issue in the debate over illegal immigration: the effect of illegal immigration on America's culture. At the most general level, *culture* can be defined as the shared values, customs, beliefs, and practices that define a group. More specifically, it refers to a group's common religion, mythology, holidays, art forms, social behaviors, political beliefs, and way of life. Traditionally, America has been viewed as having one dominant culture based on the English language, Judeo-Christian values, and Western philosophical and political ideals, such as belief in a democratic government, self-reliance, and individual rights. Throughout American history newly arrived immigrants were expected to adopt these values and customs. Although they were not required to disavow their heritage, change religion, or stop speaking their native language, they were expected to learn English, integrate themselves into American society, and throw their allegiance behind the stars and stripes. As a general rule immigrants assimilated within two generations.

"America is clearly failing to assimilate large numbers of immigrants into the mainstream of society."[28]

— Dan Stein, executive director of the Federation for American Immigration Reform.

A popular metaphor emerged to illustrate this process of assimilation, also referred to as "acculturation" or "Americanization." American society was characterized as a melting pot in which diverse peoples changed to become more similar

Transformed Neighborhoods

Residents of some neighborhoods have protested changes that they say have been brought by the arrival of illegal immigrants. Sterling Park, Virginia, a suburb of Washington, D.C., provides an example. In recent years residents have begun to complain about an influx of illegal immigrants who they say are contributing to a rise in crime, gang violence, and traffic congestion. They also cite problems such as overcrowding in single-family homes, overgrown yards, cars parked on front lawns, and unlicensed commercial vehicles parked along curbs. Eugene Delgaudio, the district supervisor for Sterling Park, summed up the frustrations felt by many residents when he stated in a radio interview: "This is not urbanization. This is a cesspool. People are coming from outside of this culture and they are dumping their [trash] on the streets of our town. And our town is outraged that they don't get with the program." Although many residents—and even the town's newspaper—dismissed Delgaudio's characterization of the town as a cesspool, many others agreed with his statements and supported his proposal to crack down on illegal immigrants.

Quoted in Sandhya Somashekhar, "Supervisor: Sterling a 'Cesspool' Due to Illegal Immigration," June 23, 2008. http://voices.washingtonpost.com.

to one another, losing the traits that set them apart and taking on the characteristics that made them alike—specifically, the English language and a respect for the nation's laws, customs, and institutions. In recent decades a competing view has emerged in which America is viewed not as a melting pot but as a tossed salad. In this metaphor diverse peoples mix together while retaining the distinct characteristics—languages and customs—that set them apart. Underlying the tossed salad metaphor is the concept of *multiculturalism*, a belief system that favors maintaining racial, ethnic, and cultural diversity within a society and its institutions (such as schools, businesses, and government agencies).

Assimilation Now

Some commentators argue that the philosophy of multiculturalism has made it easier for illegal immigrants—and other immigrants too—to resist assimilation and retain their native cultures. Most specifically, they cite public policies and educational practices that enable immigrants to retain their language rather than adopt English. J.D. Hayworth, a representative from Arizona, expresses this view:

> Americanization has given way to an insidious multiculturalism. . . . So instead of Americanization, we offer bilingual education, racial and ethnic quotas, and education that focuses not on American heroes and culture, but on a potpourri of ethnic heroes and cultures. We print multilingual ballots and driver's license tests. Schools and hospitals have government-funded—make that taxpayer-funded—translators. Immigrants are encouraged to not just preserve their language and heritage, which they should, but to have their language and heritage compete with and replace our own.[29]

Hayworth and others contend that by discouraging assimilation, these policies threaten to create social divisions and undermine the nation's civic and cultural institutions.

In addition to the theory of multiculturalism, experts cite several other major reasons for the failure of illegal immigrants to acculturate. First, many illegal immigrants do not intend to remain in the country permanently; rather, they come to America temporarily to work and earn money to take back home. Second, unlike earlier generations of Europeans and Asians, Mexicans and other Latin American immigrants have not traveled to a New World that is separated from their home by a vast ocean. The relative closeness of the United States allows the ties that bind Hispanic illegal immigrants to their homelands to remain intact. Third, the latest wave of immigrants is huge—over 11 million illegal immigrants

A bilingual sample ballot, printed in both English and Spanish, ensures that immigrants such as this man can take part in the American political process despite having limited English-language skills. Some Americans oppose bilingual help for new immigrants.

reside in the United States. Moreover, upon arrival most of these immigrants find communities and networks of people who speak their language and can assist them, thus negating their need to learn English in order to function in society. Finally, their legal status itself prevents illegal immigrants from assimilating, as it stops them from fully participating in the political and social processes that make up the culture.

Measuring Assimilation

In an effort to gain a clear picture of the process of acculturation, one researcher has attempted to put a numerical value on, or quantify, the degree to which different groups of immigrants have assimilated into mainstream American society. Jacob L. Vigdor, an associate professor of public policy and economics at Duke University, used U.S. census data from 1900 to 2006 to compare groups of immigrants to the native-born population at various times in history. He rated the similarity of immigrants to native-born people along three dimensions—economic, cultural, and civic—using a scale of 0 to 100, with 0 being completely different and 100 being identical. The economic index compared labor force, educational attainment, and home ownership patterns. The cultural index compared English-speaking ability, marriage, and childbearing patterns. Finally, the civic index compared naturalization rates and military service patterns. The three indices were also combined to form a composite index.

Vigdor found that overall the newly arrived immigrants of today are less similar to natives than were newly arrived immigrants of the early twentieth century. However, today's newly arrived immigrants assimilate faster than those of a century ago. Even so, today's rate of assimilation is lower than at any point in the twentieth century. Vigdor found that immigrants from Mexico had a composite rating of 13, the lowest of all the countries studied (Canada had the highest rating at 53). In terms of the three dimensions, Mexican immigrants experience very low rates of economic and civic assimilation, although they experience relatively normal rates of cultural assimilation. This result suggests that Mexican immigrants are learning English, marrying, and having children at rates similar to native-born Americans. However, they lag in the areas of education, income, home ownership, naturalization, and military service. Vigdor speculates that this lag is the result of the illegal status of many Mexican immigrants: "The slow rates of economic and civic assimilation set Mexicans apart from other immigrants, and may reflect the fact that the large numbers of Mexican immigrants residing in

"Hispanics are doing what American immigrants have always done: learning English, finishing school, opening their own businesses, and intermarrying with Americans."[31]

— Mortimer B. Zuckerman, editor in chief of *U.S. News & World Report.*

the United States illegally have few opportunities to advance themselves along these lines."[30]

Vigdor's study provides evidence that illegal immigrants are assimilating at a much slower rate than other immigrants. However, it does not support the claim that such immigrants do not *want* to assimilate—only that their illegal status prevents them from doing so. Mortimer B. Zuckerman, editor in chief of *U.S. News & World Report*, is one of many commentators who insist that illegal immigrants are just as eager as legal immigrants to become part of the American mainstream:

> Pervasive in the [immigration] debate is the deep fear that America is being divided into two cultures, with two languages, because of what many see as the unwillingness of Latinos, especially Mexican immigrants, to assimilate into American culture. . . . Yet the fact is Hispanics are doing what American immigrants have always done: learning English, finishing school, opening their own businesses, and intermarrying with Americans.[31]

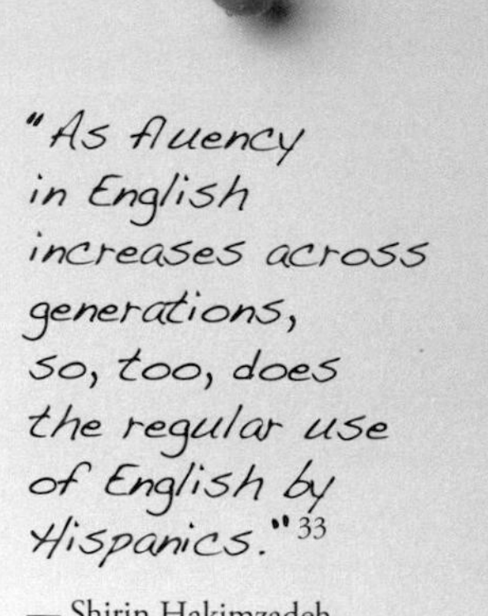

— Shirin Hakimzadeh, anthropology researcher, and D'Vera Cohn, senior writer for the Pew Hispanic Center.

The results of Vigdor's study suggest that illegal immigrants simply make this transition into American culture more slowly than other groups.

Learning English

As Zuckerman indicates, one of the main indicators of assimilation is the learning of English. The strongest opponents of illegal immigration insist that the latest wave of Latino immigrants are more inclined to retain their foreign tongue than previous waves of immigrants, who came largely from Europe. Jay Nordlinger, a senior editor for *National Review*, a conservative weekly journal, sums up this view: "The old deal was, you came to America and you assimilated into the culture. . . . You retained your mother tongue, of course, and you figured your children would know it, and you hoped your grandchildren would be interested. . . . But you were in America, and America included English." According to Nordlinger, because Hispanic im-

migrants are less likely to embrace English, they become "trapped in a linguistic ghetto—barrio-ization, some people have called it."[32]

Two young women, one from South Korea and the other from Mexico, work on their English-language reading skills. Studies show that Latin American immigrants, like other immigrants, try to learn English once they move here.

Contrary to the concerns of Nordlinger and other immigration opponents, Vigdor's study found that Mexican immigrants learn English at the same rate as other immigrants. In addition, surveys suggest that Hispanic immigrants are eager to learn English. A study by the Pew Hispanic Center, an organization that studies issues affecting Latinos in America, found that 57 percent of Latinos believe that immigrants have to speak English to be a part of American society. In addition, 92 percent of Latinos believe it is very important to teach English to the children of immigrants. Interestingly, only 2 percent of Latinos believe it is not important to teach English to the children of immigrants, whereas 27 percent of non-Latinos hold this view.

In another report the Pew Center found that only 23 percent of first-generation Latino immigrants speak English very well. However, the study also found that 88 percent of the U.S.-born children of immigrants speak English very well, and that number rises to 94 percent among later generations. The Pew Center concludes: "As fluency in English increases across generations, so, too, does the regular use of English by Hispanics, both at home and at work. For most immigrants, English is not the primary language they use in either setting. But for their grown children, it is."[33] Thus, the acquisition of English by Latino immigrants appears similar to that among previous waves of immigrants, in which proficiency was reached by the second and third generations.

Bilingual Education

The debate over illegal immigrant assimilation—especially the learning of English—is particularly intense when it touches on the nation's schools and the education of American children. In 1982 the U.S. Supreme Court ruled in *Plyler v. Doe* that it is unconstitutional to deny an education to illegal immigrant children. In addition, children born in the United States to illegal immigrant parents are U.S. citizens by birthright. According to a 2009 report by the Pew Hispanic Center, 73 percent of the children of illegal immigrants are U.S. citizens, for a total of 4 million children. The public schools are required to accommodate both illegal immigrant children and the U.S.-born children of illegal immigrant parents. Many of these children have little or no proficiency in English. These students are referred to as limited English proficiency (LEP) students, English language learners (ELLs), or simply English learners (ELs). The challenge is not only how to teach them English, but also whether to teach them other topics (such as math, science, and social studies) in Spanish, English, or some combination of both.

"Bilingual schools are capable of providing opportunities for students to achieve and sustain high levels of academic excellence even when faced with challenges such as poverty and a lack of student's English proficiency."[34]

— Norman Gold, education consultant and author.

Beginning in the 1960s bilingual education emerged as a way to address the needs of ELs. There are several models of bilingual education, but all of them adhere to the same basic idea: ELs must be taught, to some degree, in their native language as well as in English. Doing so will allow them to become literate in both languages without falling behind in their learning of crucial content such as math, science, and social studies. According to a report

Should Libraries Have Bilingual Collections?

Academics not only debate the value of bilingual education for immigrant students, but also whether libraries should contain bilingual collections. In 1988 the American Library Association, the nation's largest professional organization for librarians and libraries, adopted its Guidelines for Library Services to Hispanics. These guidelines call for librarians to create collections that meet the diverse needs of patrons, some of whom speak English, some of whom speak Spanish, and some of whom are bilingual. In response, many libraries stock their shelves with books written in both English and Spanish. "I advocate open information and accessibility for the millions of Latino citizens who work, pay taxes, and are library users,"[1] says librarian Todd Douglas Quesada. Others object to the movement to make libraries bilingual. For example, librarian Julia Stephens acknowledges that a large influx of Hispanic immigrants—both legal and illegal—"will affect the way libraries do business," but she insists that libraries must offer materials solely in English in order to help newcomers assimilate. She says, "Libraries help maintain our American identity and unity as a nation when they stock books in our common language: Standard English."[2]

1. Todd Douglas Quesada, "Spanish Spoken Here," *American Libraries*, November 2007, p. 40.
2. Julia Stephens, "English Spoken Here," *American Libraries*, November 2007, p. 43.

published by the San Diego County Office of Education, "Bilingual schools are capable of providing opportunities for students to achieve and sustain high levels of academic excellence even when faced with challenges such as poverty and a lack of student's English proficiency."[34]

Not everyone agrees with this characterization of bilingual education. Opponents contend that bilingual education impedes students' learning of English and other subjects and delays assimilation. At a more abstract level, critics cite bilingual education as yet another sign that the latest wave of Latino immigrants seeks to retain their own culture rather than embrace the American way of life. Instead of bilingual education, these commentators favor placing ELs in English language immersion programs, in which they are taught primarily in English and then quickly moved into mainstream classes taught entirely in English.

"The immigrant . . . must understand that when he comes to the U.S., swears allegiance and accepts its bounty, he undertakes to join its civic culture. In English."[37]

— Charles Krauthammer, columnist and commentator.

In the late 1990s debate over bilingual education heated up in California, the state with the largest number of ELs. In 1998 voters passed Proposition 227, which required schools to move ELs into English language immersion programs. The law allowed parents to waive their children into bilingual education classes instead of English immersion. Nevertheless, as a result of Proposition 227, within 5 years the number of ELs in bilingual education programs dropped from 30 percent to 8 percent. Following California's lead, Arizona and Massachusetts have passed similar laws. By most accounts, English immersion has not proved more effective than bilingual education. A 5-year study conducted by an independent research group found that while test scores improved slightly for English immersion students, they improved for all other students as well, including bilingual education students. The authors state, "We cannot conclude from these findings that one EL instructional service is more effective than another."[35] In other words, bilingual programs appear to be as effective as English immersion programs.

Official English

The debate over bilingual education in the schools mirrors a more general controversy over the role of English in American society. In recent years a movement has emerged to make English the official language of the United States. In fact, 30 states already have laws or constitutional amendments declaring English to be the official language within their borders. These laws do not forbid foreign-language speakers from using their native tongue. Rather, they require that all road signs, government forms, driver's license exams, and other official documents be printed only in English. Proponents insist that making English the official language will protect the country against the divisive effects of multiple languages. Organizations with names like ProEnglish and English First have emerged in an effort to make "official English" a national law.

ProEnglish is careful to define what it means—and does not mean—by "official English." The organization makes it clear that government agencies would still be allowed to use foreign languages when necessary to protect public safety, assure equality before the law, provide for national defense, and in other compelling situations. According to ProEnglish: "Having English as our official language simply means that for the government to act officially, it must communicate in English. It means the language of record is the English language."[36] Conservative columnist Charles Krauthammer, himself an immigrant (from Canada), summarizes the message official English would send to immigrants: "The immigrant, of course, has the right to speak whatever he wants. But he must understand that when he comes to the U.S., swears allegiance and accepts its bounty, he undertakes to join its civic culture. In English."[37]

The American Story

Krauthammer's words succinctly capture the views of many commentators on the illegal immigration issue. Immigration is part of the American story; however, assimilation is also part of that story. It would be misleading to say that immigrants have always been welcomed to the United States as long as they demonstrated a willingness to assimilate into the culture. Rather, as stated by Walter A. Ewing, a senior researcher at the Immigration Policy Center, a public policy research organization, "Public and political attitudes toward immigrants have always been ambivalent and contradictory, and sometimes hostile."[38] Nevertheless, despite their differences—their poor English skills and foreign beliefs and customs—immigrants have gradually been absorbed into the population and have shaped the nation's unique identity and culture. Whether one views the country as a melting pot or a tossed salad, American society is surely a hodgepodge of disparate peoples who form a distinct culture that remains the envy of much of the world.

FACTS

- As a result of the immigration protests of April and May 2006, a Zogby poll found that 32 percent of Americans were more sympathetic to the plight of undocumented workers, while 61 percent were less sympathetic.
- In California more than 15 percent of students in kindergarten through grade 12 are children of illegal immigrants. In Texas, Arizona, and Nevada, between 10 and 15 percent of students in kindergarten through grade 12 are children of illegal immigrants.
- As of 2008 the states with the largest proportion of illegal immigrants were California (25 percent), Texas (14 percent), Florida (7 percent), New York (6 percent), Arizona (5 percent), and Illinois (5 percent).
- In a 2007 *Los Angeles* Times/Bloomberg poll, 36 percent of Americans said illegal immigrants have a negative effect on community life, while 21 percent said they have a positive effect, and 29 percent were unsure whether their impact is positive or negative.
- A 2006 Rasmussen poll found that 85 percent of Americans favor legislation to make English the official language of the United States.

Does Illegal Immigration Lead to Increased Crime and Terrorism?

In March 2005 Mahmoud Youssef Kourani, a resident of Dearborn, Michigan, pleaded guilty in a Detroit federal court to providing material support to Hezbollah, a terrorist group in Lebanon.

In October 2008 police in Montgomery County, Maryland, arrested Jose Juan Garcia-Perlera, 33. Officials allege that during the previous 13 months, Garcia-Perlera had broken into several homes, hog-tied their elderly owners, and stolen their property.

In January 2009 Rony Izaguirre-Henriquez, a member of the Mara Salvatrucha (MS-13) gang, was sentenced to 30 years in prison for stabbing a teenager to death.

At first glance these three events appear to have little in common. However, upon closer inspection, it becomes clear that the crimes committed by all three of these men should never have happened on U.S. soil. All three perpetrators were illegal immigrants—Garcia-Perlera from Mexico, Izaguirre-Henriquez from El Salvador, and Kourani from Lebanon. These are just three of the many examples that opponents of illegal immigration cite to support their view that illegal immigration is a threat to the safety of citizens and the security of the nation. While the vast majority of immigrants—legal and illegal—come to America to work and build better lives for themselves, some turn to crime and some may even be terrorists bent on carrying out major acts of destruction on American soil.

Counting Illegal Immigrant Criminals

Due to their illegal status, it is difficult to know how many illegal immigrants engage in criminal activities (aside from the crime of being in the country illegally). In an attempt to measure the number of illegal immigrant criminals, the General Accountability Office counted the number of "criminal aliens" in federal, state, and local prisons and jails. The designation "criminal alien" includes both legal and illegal immigrants. The GAO found that in 2004 there were 49,000 criminal aliens in federal prisons (27 percent of the federal prison population). In 2003 there were 74,000 criminal aliens in state prisons and 147,000 criminal aliens in local facilities. Thus, taken together, it could be estimated that there are about 270,000 criminal aliens in custody in the United States. But, again, this number includes both legal and illegal immigrants.

"The problem of crime in the United States is not 'caused' or even aggravated by immigrants, regardless of their legal status."[41]

— Rubén G. Rumbaut, professor of sociology at the University of California at Irvine, and Walter A. Ewing, research associate at the Immigration Policy Center.

The Federation for American Immigration Reform, an organization that advocates reduced legal immigration and strict measures to stop illegal immigration, conducted a study to find out how many illegal immigrants—as opposed to both legal and illegal immigrants—are incarcerated. FAIR relied on data collected by the State Criminal Alien Assistance Program (SCAAP), a federal program that reimburses state and local governments for the costs of incarcerating immigrants. In 2000 the SCAAP paid for 600 million incarceration days; 24.5 million of those days were illegal immigrant days. Based on these numbers, FAIR concludes that 1 of every 22 prisoners (4.5 percent) is an illegal immigrant. By contrast, according to FAIR, 1 of every 36 adults (2.8 percent) in the country is an illegal immigrant. Because the proportion of illegal immigrants in prisons is higher than the proportion of ille-

Hightstown, New Jersey: Sanctuary City

Many cities and counties have adopted so-called sanctuary policies that forbid local police from inquiring into people's immigration status. Opponents insist that these policies hinder the federal government's enforcement of immigration laws. Supporters respond that they help local law enforcement officials fight crime by permitting illegal immigrants to report crimes against them without fear that they will be detained or deported on immigration charges. Hightstown, New Jersey, is one town that has enacted such a policy, and some illegal immigrants report that they are now more willing to cooperate with law enforcement. For example, after being mugged, Julio, an illegal immigrant from Guatemala, reported the crime to police. "They came out to meet me, made a report and gave me a ride home," Julio said. "They haven't caught the guys who did it, but at least I didn't feel like I was the one who committed a crime."

Quoted in *Washington Post*, "Looking the Other Way on Immigrants," April 10, 2007, p, A1.

gal immigrants in the general population, FAIR concludes that illegal immigrants are more prone to crime than other people: "It is this greater likelihood of being incarcerated that clearly demonstrates that illegal aliens are disproportionately involved in criminal activity."[39]

An Immigrant Crime Wave?

To gain a clearer picture of the illegal immigrant prisoner population, the GAO studied a group of 55,322 incarcerated immigrants whom U.S. Immigration and Customs Enforcement had determined to be illegal immigrants. The GAO concluded that these 55,322 inmates were arrested a total of 459,614 times, an average of 8 times each. In addition, they were arrested for a total of about 700,000 different offenses, an average of about 13 offenses each.

Of these offenses, 45 percent were drug or immigration crimes; 15 percent were property crimes such as car theft, burglary, or property damage; and 12 percent were violent offenses, including robbery, assault, murder, and rape. The remaining 28 percent were weapons violations, driving under the influence, fraud, and obstruction of justice.

Taken together these statistics suggest that at least a segment of the illegal immigrant population is placing a heavy burden on society by victimizing legitimate residents and requiring large criminal justice costs for their capture and incarceration. According to journalist R. Cort Kirkwood: "Illegal aliens [are] brutalizing Americans in a crime wave of unfathomable proportions. They are robbing Americans. They are raping Americans. They are murdering Americans."[40] While this statement might strike some as an exaggeration, people who have been victimized by a person in the country illegally would most likely agree with the sentiment behind it.

More Immigrants Equals Less Crime?

Some economists, sociologists, and criminologists have used different methods to study the illegal immigrant prison population and have come up with conclusions that differ from those of FAIR. Kristin F. Butcher, an associate professor of economics at Wellesley College, and Anne Morrison Piehl, an associate professor of economics and criminal justice at Rutgers University, used census data from 1980 to 2000 and concluded that immigrants are one-fifth as likely as native-born residents to be incarcerated. However, these researchers did not differentiate between legal and illegal immigrants.

Rubén G. Rumbaut, a professor of sociology at the University of California at Irvine, and Walter A. Ewing, a research associate at the Immigration Policy Center, a think tank that focuses on immigration, studied the relationship between immigration and crime and came to the same conclusion as Butcher and Piehl. They found that in 2000 the incarceration rate for men between the ages of 18 and 39 was 5 times higher for the native-born than the foreign-born. Foreign-born Mexicans were 8 times less likely to be incarcerated than native-born men of

Mexican descent. Foreign-born Salvadoran and Guatemalan men were 6 times less likely to be incarcerated than native-born men of Salvadoran and Guatemalan descent. The incarceration rates of Chinese, Laotian, and other Asian immigrants were equally low. Based on their findings Rumbaut and Ewing conclude, "The problem of crime in the United States is not 'caused' or even aggravated by immigrants, regardless of their legal status." In fact, as they point out, "even as the undocumented population has doubled to 12 million since 1994, the violent crime rate has fallen 26.4 percent."[41]

"Some gangs—the 18th Street Gang and Mara Salvatrucha (or MS-13), for example—are believed to have a largely illegal membership."[44]

—Jessica M. Vaughan, senior policy analyst for the Center for Immigration Studies, and Jon D. Feere, legal policy analyst at the Center for Immigration Studies.

One researcher goes so far as to say that immigration reduces crime. Robert J. Sampson, a professor of sociology at Harvard University, has studied the relationship between immigration and crime since the 1990s. Like Rumbaut and Ewing he points out that violent crime has decreased during the most recent wave of immigration—much of it illegal immigration from Mexico. In addition, he studied violent crime in Chicago and found that rates of violence among Mexican Americans were much lower than among either blacks or whites. Based on these findings, he concludes, the massive influx of Hispanic immigrants—legal and illegal—has actually helped reduce the rate of violent crime in America: "Immigration—even if illegal—is associated with *lower* crime rates in most disadvantaged neighborhoods."[42]

Different theories are offered to explain the statistics showing a relationship between illegal immigration and low crime rates. Some suggest that the low crime rates reflect the fact that illegal immigrants are reluctant to report crimes against them because they fear attracting the attention of law enforcement and immigration officials. Others insist that illegal immigrants refrain from committing crimes for the same reason. As stated by Robert F. Mulligan, an associate professor of economics at Western Carolina University, "Illegal immigrants may be deterred from criminality by the relatively high penalty of deportation for even minor crimes."[43] Unfortunately, this aversion to crime is not passed down to the U.S.-born children of immigrants, who are much more likely to engage in crime than their foreign-born parents.

Illegal Immigrant Gang Crime

Despite the uncertainty regarding the number of incarcerated illegal immigrants and the impact of illegal immigration on the crime rate, the fact remains that there are more than 11 million illegal immigrants in the country, and some of them engage in criminal activity. Of greatest concern to law enforcement officials is the threat posed by illegal immigrant gang members. Throughout history many immigrants, facing poverty and few economic opportunities, have been drawn to gangs in order to attain economic and social security. Recent arrivals are no exception. The gangs with the largest number of immigrant members—including illegal immigrants—are Hispanic gangs such as Mara Salvatrucha (MS-13), Sureños-13, and the 18th Street Gang. According to an October 2008 report by the Center for Immigration Studies, an organization that favors reduced immigration and strong control of the

Posters of arrested gang members are displayed in Washington, D.C., in 2007. Under Operation Community Shield, gangs with illegal immigrant members were targeted for arrest. Nearly half of those arrested between 2005 and 2007 were members of MS-13 and Sureños-13.

border, "Some gangs—the 18th Street Gang and Mara Salvatrucha (or MS-13), for example—are believed to have a largely illegal membership."[44]

Of the various gangs with illegal immigrant members, by far the most notorious is MS-13, which originated among immigrants fleeing civil war and economic hardship in Central America—primarily El Salvador—in the 1980s and 1990s. Because these immigrants came from war-torn countries, they were desensitized to mayhem and adapted to America's inner-city gang culture with gusto, often using machetes and paramilitary tactics to carry out acts of grisly violence. According to the report by the CIS, there are 10,000 members of MS-13 spread throughout 48 states, the District of Columbia, and Puerto Rico. In addition, due in part to massive deportations of Salvadorans in the late 1990s and early 2000s, the gang has spread throughout Central America and Mexico, and MS-13 now controls many of the routes by which drugs and illegal aliens are smuggled into the country across the Mexican border. It is estimated that between 60 and 90 percent of MS-13 members are illegal immigrants.

Although there may be disagreement concerning the numbers of illegal immigrant criminals and gang members, there is no disputing the viciousness of MS-13. Numerous anecdotal accounts of machete attacks, gang rapes, murder, and witness intimidation can be found in the nation's newspapers. As the CIS reports: "MS-13 strives to be the most violent and feared gang in the world. Activities vary from one location to another, but members have been convicted of such crimes as murder, murder for hire, assault, extortion, kidnapping, theft, retail drug dealing, prostitution, rape, home invasion, robbery, burglary, and numerous other crimes."[45]

Much of the violence perpetrated by MS-13 is directed at rival gang members, the CIS explains, but many of the gang's crimes are inflicted on ordinary citizens, with the largest burden falling on the immigrant community: "Immigrant business owners experience gang-related burglary, extortion, and vandalism. Immigrant children are considered ripe targets for gang recruitment and are sometimes threatened for refusing to join."[46]

Combating Illegal Immigrant Gangs

Some critics maintain that the problem of illegal immigrant gang violence is made worse by the existence of sanctuary policies in many major cities, including Los Angeles, San Francisco, New York, and Miami. These laws forbid police officers from inquiring about a suspect's immigration status. The purpose of sanctuary laws is to encourage illegal immigrants to cooperate with local law enforcement authorities without fear of deportation. However, critics charge that the laws prevent the police from getting criminal illegal immigrant gang members off the streets. Heather Mac Donald, a senior fellow at the Manhattan Institute, a public policy research organization, cites several instances in which illegal immigrant gang members have been in police custody only to be set free because officers could not check their immigration status. She concludes that "sanctuary laws are a serious impediment to stemming gang violence and other crime. Moreover, they are a perfect symbol of this country's topsy-turvy stance toward illegal immigration."[47]

"There are hundreds of illegal aliens apprehended entering the United States each year who are from countries known to support and sponsor terrorism."[50]

— Majority Staff of the House Committee on Homeland Security Subcommittee on Investigations.

Despite the existence of sanctuary policies, ICE has made some progress in combating illegal immigrant gangs in recent years. Since 1995 ICE has undertaken Operation Community Shield (OCS), in which federal agents have teamed up with local law enforcement agencies to identify and arrest gang members for immigration violations. ICE agents have greater authority to question suspects than do local law enforcement officials. They also have an easier time getting permission to enter and search residences without a warrant. These abilities help them to gather information about gang membership and criminal activities that can assist in the arrest and prosecution of gang members. As a result of OCS, ICE arrested more than 8,000 gang members from 2005 to 2007. Nearly half of them were members of MS-13 or Sureños-13; 60 percent were Mexicans, 17 percent were from El Salvador, 5 percent were from Honduras, and the rest were from Guatemala, Jamaica, and elsewhere. While OCS represents a major success in the fight against illegal gang crime, arrests were low in cities and states with sanctuary laws, such as Los Angeles and Oregon, despite the large number of gang members in those regions.

The Threat of Illegal Immigrant Terrorists

In addition to committing crimes and forming gangs, critics argue, illegal immigrants also pose a threat to national security. Experts point out that 4 of the 19 perpetrators of the September 11, 2001, attacks on America were in the country illegally (their visas had expired). Indeed, in the wake of the attacks, which killed nearly 3,000 people, government leaders undertook a thorough review of

Illegal Immigrant Drunk Drivers

On Christmas Eve 2006 Carlos Rodolfo Prieto, an unlicensed illegal immigrant from Mexico, was driving in Salt Lake City, Utah, when he ran a red light and crashed into a car carrying a family of 6. The mother, Cheryl Ceran, and 2 of her children were killed; the father, Gary, and 2 other children survived. Prieto also survived, and when tested by police, he failed a roadside sobriety test and admitted he had drunk 5 beers before getting behind the wheel. The Ceran tragedy is one of many stories that are cited as evidence that illegal immigrants are involved in a disproportionate number of fatal drunk-driving accidents. Researchers have found that the states with the highest number of illegal immigrant residents also have the highest number of fatal hit-and-run crashes. This correlation does not necessarily prove that illegal immigrants cause a greater number of accidents. Yet proponents of stronger immigration laws conclude that, coupled with the many horrific stories like the Cerans', it is evidence that the country should increase its efforts to keep illegal immigrants out of the country and off the nation's highways.

Illegal immigrants are searched by U.S. immigration and customs officials in Arizona. Hundreds of thousands of illegal immigrants are apprehended each year while trying to unlawfully enter the country.

the nation's immigration policies and instituted new procedures in an attempt to prevent a similar attack from occurring in the future. By most accounts it is now more difficult for potential terrorists to enter the country, either legally or illegally. However, many critics contend that the policy changes have not gone far enough and that the potential still exists for terrorists to enter the country illegally and carry out attacks on U.S. soil.

Immigration opponents fear that terrorists may enter the country alongside illegal immigrants who are simply looking for work. As stated in a 2008 FAIR report, "The assumption must be made that as long as individuals can sneak into the United States or hire smugglers to get them into the country, those routes of entry are available to members of al-Qaeda or other terrorist organizations."[48] Indeed, each year U.S. Customs and Border Protection (CBP), the division of the Department of Homeland Security that controls the border, apprehends hundreds of thousands of illegal immigrants attempting to enter the country. The majority are Mexicans (89 percent in 2007). However, many are from countries other than Mexico, including nations designated "special-interest" countries. These include countries that the U.S. government believes are intent on exporting terrorism, such as Iran, Yemen, and Lebanon. From 2001 through the first half of 2005, officials captured 91,516 immigrants from these countries.

The nation's overloaded immigration system contributes to the problem posed by immigrants from special-interest countries. These immigrants cannot be shipped home as easily as Mexicans, and there are not enough detention beds to hold them. Therefore, many are released with a summons to report back in several weeks for a deportation hearing. However, the vast majority simply disappear. Of the 91,516 apprehended between 2001 and the first half of 2005, 45,000 (49 percent) were released into the U.S. population. In addition, the GAO reports that in 2006 several thousand "inadmissible aliens and other violators" slipped past CBP officials at air and land ports of entry. "When CBP does not apprehend a potentially dangerous person," the GAO concludes, "this increases the potential that national security may be compromised."[49]

Many government officials are concerned about the terrorist threat posed by such illegal immigrants at large inside the nation's borders. In 2006 the Majority Staff of the House Committee on Homeland Security Subcommittee on Investigations issued a report detailing various criminal and terrorist incursions along the southwestern border of the United States. Among the report's warnings are the following claims:

> There are hundreds of illegal aliens apprehended entering the United States each year who are from countries known to support and sponsor terrorism. . . . Aliens were smuggled from the Middle East to staging areas in Central

and South America before being smuggled into the United States. Members of Hezbollah have already entered the United States across the Southwest border.[50]

It is important to note that this report was not bipartisan. In fact, it was condemned by the chair and several Democratic members of the Homeland Security Committee, who characterized the report as "inflammatory, uncorroborated, and partisan."[51] However, the Majority Staff's report reflects the views of many political leaders and commentators who believe that the southern border is too vulnerable to terrorists who seek to do harm to the United States.

Disputing the Link Between Immigration and Terrorism

While some politicians and pundits believe there is a strong connection between illegal immigration and the threat of terrorism, others reject this link. These commentators point out that the September 11 attacks were not carried out by illegal border crossers. Rather, the attackers had all entered the country legally using visas. As stated by Payan, those who analyzed the security failure that led to the attacks "focused on border openness in Arizona and New Mexico as a fundamental problem that contributed to September 11, in spite of the fact that the border had hardly anything to do with the terrorist attacks."[52] Although four of the hijackers had allowed their visas to lapse, this fact highlights the need to reform the visa system, not to clamp down at the border.

Rather than illegal immigration, Payan and others insist, the blame for the September 11 attacks lies in the U.S. intelligence community's failure to anticipate and prevent the hijackings. Focusing on illegal immigration as a possible cause of terrorism could actually do more harm than good, because it may distract government officials from the more important work of improving intelligence gathering and antiterror measures. Edward Alden, a journalist and the author of *The Closing of the American*

Border: Terrorism, Immigration, and Security Since 9/11, argues that immigration and terrorism both need to be addressed, but as individual problems: "We need to separate the debates on terrorism and immigration. There are very serious debates to be had about both, but conflating the two does a disservice to both."[53]

"We need to separate the debates on terrorism and immigration. There are very serious debates to be had about both, but conflating the two does a disservice to both."[53]

— Edward Alden, author of *The Closing of the American Border: Terrorism, Immigration, and Security Since 9/11.*

Perhaps surprisingly, FAIR agrees that immigration and terrorism are largely separate issues; however, the organization insists that the two issues do overlap and must be considered together: "The issue of national security is much broader than just the immigration-related aspects, and the issue of immigration policy and enforcement is much broader than the aspects that relate to national security, but there is a very large area of overlap between the two."[54]

Balancing Fear and Hope

Although experts debate the link between illegal immigration and terrorism, many people are concerned that the large numbers of illegal immigrants entering the country each year, along with the more than 11 million already living in the country, pose a threat to the nation's safety and security. In the debate over numbers—the number of incarcerated illegal immigrants, the number of crimes committed by illegal immigrants, the number of illegal immigrants from special-interest countries—it is easy to lose sight of what is at stake. One hit-and-run drunk driver can devastate a family. One rape, one murder, one burglary can cause trauma that will last a lifetime. One terrorist act can leave an entire nation in mourning and shaky with fear.

Although the vast majority of illegal immigrants come to America to pursue the American Dream, some in fact cause nightmares due to the crimes they commit, while still others may seek to spread large-scale violence and panic. The challenge for Americans is to balance their need to protect themselves against violence and fear while staying true to their values of openness, tolerance, and hope for a future of peace and prosperity.

FACTS

- A 2008 New Jersey study found that illegal immigrants were 50 percent as likely as U.S. citizens to end up in jail.

- As the illegal immigrant population doubled between 1994 and 2004, the rate of violent crime decreased by 35.1 percent, according to the Immigration Policy Center.

- A 2007 Rasmussen poll found that 58 percent of Americans support cutting off federal funding to cities that have sanctuary policies, which prevent local law enforcement from reporting illegal immigrants to federal officials.

- The Mara Salvatrucha (MS-13) gang gets its name from the Spanish *mara* ("group of young people" or "mob"), *salva* (a reference to El Salvador), and *trucha* ("on guard"). The number 13 represents the letter M in the alphabet and signifies an allegiance to the Mexican Mafia, a Southern California prison gang.

- In its 2005 Gang Threat Assessment, the U.S. Department of Justice found little evidence of any connections between immigrant gangs and international terrorist groups.

- According to a 2007 *New York Times*/CBS poll, 53 percent of Americans believe illegal immigrants are as likely as others to commit crimes, while 30 percent believe they are more likely, and 14 percent believe they are less likely to commit crimes.

How Should the Government Respond to Illegal Immigration?

In December 2005 the House of Representatives passed an immigration reform bill called the Border Protection, Antiterrorism, and Illegal Immigration Control Act. The bill called for tighter border controls and enforcement of laws against hiring illegal immigrants. In perhaps its most controversial provision, the bill would have made it illegal to knowingly aid an illegal immigrant in any way. The bill passed with strong Republican support. However, it sparked mass protests by immigrants and their supporters, who believed the measure was too harsh.

In May 2006 the U.S. Senate passed a separate bill dubbed the Comprehensive Immigration Reform Act. Like the House bill, the Senate bill called for new border efforts to control illegal immigration. However, the Senate bill also included a process to allow illegal immigrants already in the country to attain legal status and a "blue card" program to increase the number of guest workers. Although the Senate bill had the support of Republican president George W. Bush and several Republican senators, including Arizona senator John McCain, many Republicans roundly rejected the bill's legalization component, which they labeled "amnesty." Due to the controversy the immigration proposals created, the two bills were never reconciled, and the government failed to find a workable solution to the illegal immigration issue.

The 2005–2006 immigration reform debacle illustrates how difficult it is to for a nation as politically diverse as the United States to deal with the problem of illegal immigration. While most people agree that the border needs to be controlled and the number of illegal entrants needs to be reduced, vast differences of opinion exist on how to reach these goals. Moreover, experts and laypersons alike disagree over what to do about the estimated 11 million illegal immigrants who are already in the country living and working alongside legal residents. Numerous proposals are put forth and debated—all of which are intended to stop illegal immigrants from entering the country, remove them or encourage them to leave once they are here, or remove the incentives that cause them to leave their homelands and venture to the United States.

Controlling the Border

Most agree that the border cannot simply be left wide open for people to come and go as they please. However, there is disagreement over the degree of enforcement that is needed at the border, the best tactics to use, and whether the benefits of heavy enforcement are worth the costs. U.S. Customs and Border Protection spent over $8 billion in 2008, and that number was expected to exceed $9.4 billion in 2009. As of 2007 there were over 18,000 Border Patrol agents monitoring the border with increasingly high-tech surveillance tools, including helicopters, cameras with night-vision capabilities, massive floodlights, underground sensors, infrared goggles, and M16 rifles.

One symbol of the debate over efforts to control the border is the border fence. In 2006 Congress passed the Secure Fence Act, a law that authorized $3 billion for the construction of 670 miles (1,078km) of fencing at heavily trafficked portions of the U.S.-Mexico border. According to the Department of Homeland Security, 553 miles (890km) of fencing had been constructed by December 19, 2008. In urban areas the fencing has 3 layers, including a layer of steel and subsequent layers of chain-link and barbed wire. While the Department of Homeland Security insists that this fencing is an essential tool in the battle against illegal immigration, the project has its critics. Environmentalists are concerned that the fence construction has damaged sensitive habitats. Others contend that it has cut border communities in half. Still others insist that it is too costly for the slight benefits it will bring. Illegal immigrants will not be denied entry; they will merely be inconvenienced. According to Chad Foster, the mayor of the border community of Eagle Pass, Texas: "This fencing will only slow an illegal entry down three to four minutes. . . . Maintaining it for 20 years will cost the taxpayers in excess of $49 billion. It makes no sense."[55]

The Secure Fence Act of 2006

In the fall of 2006 President Bush signed a bill approving the construction of fencing along the U.S.-Mexico border. In addition to the fencing, the bill includes the implementation of other security measures such as cameras, lighting, and sensors. Critics claim that increased fencing will slow down illegal crossings but not prevent them.

Source: CNN.com, "Secure Fence Act of 2006," 2006. www.cnn.com.

As a result of its various border control efforts, the CBP apprehended over 850,000 illegal border crossers and arrested more than 25,000 criminals at ports of entry in 2007. Nevertheless, it is estimated that as many 500,000 illegal immigrants continue to enter the country each year. To some, these statistics prove that more border security is needed; to others, they reveal that border security is largely futile and that the problem of illegal immigration must be solved by other means. As stated by Payan, "The steel fences, the cameras, the Humvees, the helicopters, the hovercrafts, the ATVs, [the] fixed-wing aircraft, etc., have not stopped the flood of undocumented workers."[56]

"The steel fences, the cameras, the Humvees, the helicopters, the hovercrafts, the ATVs, [the] fixed-wing aircraft, etc., have not stopped the flood of undocumented workers."[52]

— Tony Payan, assistant professor of international relations and foreign policy at the University of Texas at El Paso.

Removing Incentives

In addition to attempting to control the border, experts call for ending various incentives that lure illegal immigrants to America. Proposals include elimination of emergency health care, education, driver's licenses (in states that permit illegal immigrants to obtain them), birthright citizenship for the children of illegal immigrant parents, and other benefits that illegal immigrants currently receive. However, perhaps the most crucial incentive is employment. The primary reason most immigrants make the journey to America is to find work that pays more than they can earn at home. Therefore, many argue, the best way to prevent illegal immigration is to make it impossible for illegal immigrants to find jobs. Once word gets out that there is no work in America, the theory goes, potential immigrants will stay at home rather than make the difficult trip to a new country.

Laws against employing illegal immigrants have existed for decades. However, these laws are inconsistently enforced and are routinely violated, especially in the agriculture and textile industries, which require large numbers of low-skilled workers. Therefore, one solution that many critics advocate is to clamp down on employers who knowingly hire illegal immigrants. In recent years U.S. Immigration and Customs Enforcement has done just that, raiding numerous companies suspected of employing illegal immigrants. In March 2007 ICE raided the Michael Bianco factory, a garment company in New Bedford, Massachusetts, and arrested 360 illegal immigrants, along with the owner and 3 managers. In February 2008 ICE agents raided Universal Industrial Sales in Lindon, Utah, and arrested 57 illegal immigrants. They also arrested the human resources director, who subsequently pleaded guilty to two counts of encouraging or inducing illegal aliens to reside in the United States unlawfully, a crime punishable by up to 10 years in prison.

Workplace enforcement operations sometimes break up elaborate illegal immigrant labor rings. For example, in February 2008 South Dakota hotel owners Robert and Angelita Farrell

Workers assemble garments at the Michael Bianco factory in New Bedford, Massachusetts, about two weeks after federal immigration and customs officers raided the factory. The officers arrested 360 illegal immigrants, the owner, and three managers.

The Environmental Impact of the Border Fence

Environmentalists are concerned that the fence being built along the U.S.-Mexico border could have devastating consequences for wildlife in the region. They are especially worried about the mountainous area that straddles southwestern Arizona in the United States and northeastern Sonora in Mexico. This region, known as Sky Island, is home to black bears, mountain lions, coatis (a relative of the raccoon), and exotic birds and snakes. As stated by science writer Michelle Nijhuis, experts fear that construction of a fence through this territory could harm wildlife by dividing species into separate populations:

> Solid fencing . . . would fragment habitat not only for large mammals such as the jaguar but also for the coati, two species of skunks, and the tiny Coues deer, a subspecies of white-tailed deer, called "the gray ghost" for its ability to seemingly vanish into the landscape. Because populations divided by the fence would have smaller pools of prospective mates, their genetic diversity—and, with it, their ability to withstand disease, environmental stresses, and other challenges—is likely to erode.

Michelle Nijhuis, "The Borderlands: Dead End," *Audubon*, September/October 2007. www.audubonmagazine.org.

were sentenced to several years for multiple charges, including visa fraud, peonage (involuntary servitude), and conspiracy. The couple had recruited illegal immigrants from the Philippines using fraudulent visas and then forced them to work 16 to 18 hours a day. "The conditions of servitude that these victims were forced to endure were simply unacceptable in any modern-day society,"[57] said Marty Jackley, U.S. attorney for the District of South Dakota.

In another case, in December 2008 six men in several cities were arrested for operating a network of staffing businesses that employed more than 100 illegal immigrants from eastern Europe—specifically, Russia, Ukraine, Estonia, and Lithuania. The Department of Homeland Security lauds such efforts as a necessary weapon in the battle against illegal immigration. As Michael Chertoff, the former secretary of the Department of Homeland Security, states, "These are the kinds of cases that have high impact on those who would hire and employ undocumented and illegal aliens, often facilitated through identity and document fraud."[58]

Immigrant-rights activists strongly criticize the ICE workplace raids. Of special concern is the impact that the raids have on the children of the illegal immigrant parents who are arrested. Many of the children, having been born on American soil, are U.S. citizens. Following the New Bedford raid, numerous news articles criticized ICE's tactics, making special note of the separation of mothers from their children. John Kerry, a Democratic senator, called for an investigation into the raid. In 2007 a report by the National Council of La Raza, a Hispanic-rights organization, and the Urban Institute, a public policy research organization, detailed the harmful effects of immigration raids on children and families:

> After the arrest or disappearance of their parents, children experienced feelings of abandonment and showed symptoms of emotional trauma, psychological duress, and mental health problems. Many lacked stability in child care and supervision. Families continued hiding and feared arrest if they ventured outside, increasing social isolation over time. Immigrant communities faced the fear of future raids, backlash from nonimmigrants, and the stigma of being labeled "illegal." The combination of fear, isolation, and economic hardship induced mental health problems such as depression, separation anxiety disorder, post-traumatic stress disorder, and suicidal thoughts.[59]

During a 2008 demonstration in Washington, D.C., protesters display a hand-painted banner that calls on federal authorities to stop illegal immigrant raids. The raids usually lead to deportations and sometimes separate parents from their U.S.-born children.

Critics such as the National Council of La Raza and the Urban Institute have called for congressional oversight of ICE's enforcement actions to ensure that children are protected and that immigrants' due process rights are not violated.

State and Local Efforts

In addition to the various federal efforts to seal the border, remove incentives, and crack down on illegal immigrant workers, state and local governments have recently begun to take their own steps to address the problem. This trend is novel and controversial; immigration has traditionally been viewed as the responsibility of the federal government. However, due to the failure of Congress to pass comprehensive immigration reform in 2006 and every year since then, state and local governments have increasingly decided that they must take matters into their own hands. "As the federal government has proved itself incapable of formulating an immigration policy," the *Economist* reports, "local governments are stepping up."[60]

Examples of state and local measures to fight illegal immigration are numerous. In 2006 Colorado passed a law denying most state benefits to illegal immigrants over the age of 18. Also in 2006 the town of Hazelton, Pennsylvania, passed an ordinance that fines landlords $1000 for each illegal immigrant they rent to. And in 2007 Arizona passed a law that imposed penalties on employers who hire illegal immigrants. Laws such as these often face challenges in court on the grounds that they are unconstitutional. However, state and local leaders, strapped for cash and finding little or no relief from the federal government, appear committed to tightening the screws on illegal immigrants themselves. In 2008, according to the National Conference of State Legislators, 1,305 immigration-related bills were considered in 45 different states; 206 of these bills were enacted into law (32 laws related to driver's licenses, 19 to employment, 12 to law enforcement, and 12 to education).

Another example of state and local involvement in the issue of illegal immigration is taking place in the arena of law enforcement. Local law enforcement actions can either impede or assist federal immigration control attempts. Some cities and localities (including Los Angeles, California; Phoenix, Arizona; and Denver, Colorado) have sanctuary policies, which forbid law enforcement officers to inquire into a suspect's immigration status. In these instances local policies hinder immigration control efforts.

> "After the arrest or disappearance of their parents, children experienced feelings of abandonment and showed symptoms of emotional trauma, psychological duress, and mental health problems."[59]
>
> — National Council of La Raza, a Hispanic civil rights organization, and the Urban Institute, a public policy research organization.

However, in other locations local law enforcement personnel partner with federal officials to address the problem of illegal immigration. Recently, immigration officials have begun using a little-known law to assist them in this effort. Section 287(g) of the 1996 Illegal Immigration Reform and Immigrant Responsibility Act (IIRIRA) allows counties and cities to sign agreements with ICE in order to receive funding for training, access to immigration databases, and money for increased detention space. In return they are asked to monitor the immigration status of people stopped by the police. As of the fall of 2008,

63 localities in 18 states received funding under this portion of the act. Many civil libertarians charge that these local immigration enforcement operations have led to racial profiling and the deportation of legal immigrants by improperly trained police officers. However, supporters claim that they are an essential tool in the fight against illegal immigration.

Deportation Versus Amnesty

Efforts to control the border, remove incentives, enforce employment laws, and crack down at state and local levels can keep some illegal immigrants from crossing the border, deter some from attempting to cross, and remove some who have already crossed. However, they cannot wholly address the presence of the more than 11 million illegal immigrants who are estimated to be living on American soil. Very few commentators believe it is possible, or even desirable, to deport such a monumental number of people. Even conservative opponents of mass *legal* immigration, who are among those most worried about the negative effects of illegal immigration on the country, concede that mass deportation would be impractical, exorbitant, and disruptive to society and the economy. This view is summed up by conservative columnist George F. Will:

> Of the nation's illegal immigrants . . . , 60 percent have been here at least five years. Most have roots in their communities. Their children born here are U.S. citizens. We are not going to take the draconian police measures necessary to deport 11 million people. They would fill 200,000 buses in a caravan stretching bumper-to-bumper from San Diego to Alaska. . . . And there are no plausible incentives to get the 11 million to board the buses.[61]

Will is among the few conservatives—joined by mostly liberals—who favor some form of legalization as outlined in the Senate bill and endorsed by former president George W. Bush.

Most advocates of legalizing the 11 million illegal immigrants currently residing in the United States are careful to make clear that they do not favor amnesty—automatically forgiving illegal immigrants for their crime and granting them legal residency. In fact, critics who labeled the legalization provision in the 2006 Senate bill an "amnesty" were either misinformed or intentionally misleading. By painting the bill with the brush of amnesty, they associated it with the 1986 Immigration Reform and Control Act (IRCA), which included an amnesty provision. Critics believe that this granting of amnesty to illegal immigrants sent a message to potential future immigrants that they would eventually be rewarded for entering the country illegally. Thus, they credit IRCA for contributing to the swell of illegal immigrants that came to the United States in subsequent years.

"We are not going to take the draconian police measures necessary to deport 11 million people."[61]

— George F. Will, conservative columnist, journalist, and author.

The legalization most commentators propose in no way resembles the amnesty of 1986, however. Illegal immigrants would be required to take various steps and wait up to a decade to achieve legal status. Among other expectations, the 2006 Senate bill endorsed by Bush would have required them to undergo background checks and security clearances, pay back taxes, learn civics and English, work steadily for years, and return to their homeland to wait in line behind other applicants for legal entry. During his campaign and soon after being elected, President Barack Obama advocated a legalization plan similar to that of Bush as part of his proposal for comprehensive immigration reform. Speaking at a town hall meeting in Costa Mesa, California, in March 2009, he explained that along with controlling the border and cracking down on employers, the nation needs to provide a way for illegal immigrants to become citizens:

> You've got to . . . say to the undocumented workers . . . you've broken the law; you didn't come here the way you were supposed to. So this is not going to be a free ride. It's not going to be some instant amnesty. What's going to happen is you are going to pay a significant fine. You are going to learn English. You are going to . . . go to the back of the line so that you don't get ahead of somebody who was in Mexico City applying legally. But after you've done these things over a certain period of time you can earn your citizenship.[62]

President Barack Obama comments on U.S. immigration policy during a town hall meeting in Costa Mesa, California, in March 2009. Obama said the United States should provide a way for illegal immigrants to become citizens—after a reasonable waiting period.

Proponents insist that this process would help to bring illegal immigrants out of the shadows to become more integrated into society. In addition, they argue, it would lead to improved wages and working conditions for low-skill workers because employers would be forced to adhere to wage and labor standards. Moreover, because immigrants would now be required to pay income taxes, more tax revenues would be available at the federal and state levels.

Attrition Through Enforcement

Experts agree that no one action can solve the problem of illegal immigration. Most propose some combination of measures. The differences are often a matter of degree and emphasis, reflecting the individual's view regarding the seriousness of the issue and the harmfulness of illegal immigration. Many of those who are adamantly opposed to large-scale immigration and who view illegal immigration as a serious threat to the country propose a policy of attrition through enforcement—that is, shrinking the illegal immigration population by strongly enforcing all existing immigration laws. These commentators insist that such strict enforcement will keep illegal border crossers out and deter others from trying to enter. In addition, far from being given a path to legality, the illegal immigrants who are already in the country should be made as uncomfortable as possible (through raids, the denial of services, and even increased deportations) so that they will either be forced out or choose to leave on their own. Mark Krikorian, a chief proponent of this view, explains that each year, many illegal immigrants decide to return home for various reasons; increasing the pressure on them can increase this number. Krikorian says, "There is a good deal of turnover in the illegal population, which we can use to our advantage."[63] He summarizes his plan as follows:

> Shrink the illegal population through consistent, across-the-board enforcement of immigration law. By deterring the settlement of new illegals, by increasing deportations to the extent possible, and most important, by increasing the number of illegals already here who give up and leave on their own, the United States can bring about an annual decrease in the illegal-alien population rather than allowing it to continually increase. . . . The result would be a shrinking of the illegal population over time to the status of a manageable nuisance rather than a crisis.[64]

"Shrink the illegal population through consistent, across-the-board enforcement of immigration law."[64]

— Mark Krikorian, executive director of the Center for Immigration Studies.

Krikorian contends that there is evidence to support his theory. The most recent numbers show that the illegal immigrant population is shrinking (from 12.5 million in August 2007 to 11.2 million in July 2008), a change he attributes to the stepped-up enforcement of recent years.

Other commentators prefer a less harsh approach to the issue. Even many of those who favor controlling the border take a more sympathetic view of the illegal immigrants who are already residing within the nation's borders. Ramesh Ponnuru, a senior editor at the conservative journal *National Review*, agrees with Krikorian's proposal up to a point. However, he suggests that once the number of immigrants has been reduced to

An Arduous Process

One common argument against illegal immigrants is that they should wait their turn to enter the country legally. However, the process for immigrating and obtaining U.S. citizenship is daunting. First, the only people currently eligible for legal entry are those with family members already legally in the county or those with skills that are needed in the U.S. workforce. Parents, spouses, and minor children of U.S. citizens can obtain a green card quite easily and can complete the process to become a citizen within 6 to 7 years. Adult children and siblings of U.S. citizens must wait 6 to 15 years to obtain a green card and 12 to 28 years to become a citizen. Relatives of lawful permanent residents must wait 5 to 14 years to get a green card and 11 to 20 years for citizenship. Skilled workers typically must have a job offer and an employer willing to do paperwork and pay fees, and they must typically wait 6 to 10 years to get a green card and 11 to 16 years to become a citizen. While the reality of legal immigration does not justify breaking the law to cross the border without permission, it helps to explain why so many choose to bypass the legal process.

a manageable number, "an amnesty might be conceivable: but only after it was clear that it would not act as an invitation to further border crossings."[65]

Thomas Wenski, the Catholic bishop of Orlando, Florida, and a consultant to the U.S. Conference of Catholic Bishops, responds from a more liberal position. He argues that the border fence, workplace raids, local law enforcement measures, and other policies have created an atmosphere of fear in immigrant communities that will do little to solve the issue of illegal immigration:

While some organizations that oppose immigration . . . hope such an atmosphere will lead to a mass exodus of illegal and legal immigrants, they are likely to be disappointed. . . . These people identify themselves more as Americans than anything else and would rather live here in the shadows than take their U.S.-citizen children back to a place they do not know.[66]

Wenski and others who share his views are more likely to support a policy by which illegal immigrants can achieve legal status.

The Bigger Picture

Still other commentators insist that all of the measures debated in the public policy arena miss the mark because they ignore the underlying cause of most illegal immigration: dire poverty in Mexico and Central America compared with the relative wealth of the United States. As stated by Joan B. Anderson, a professor of economics at the University of San Diego, and James Gerber, a professor of economics at San Diego State University, "It is difficult to identify any other countries in the world sharing a common border that have income differences as large as those between the United States and Mexico."[67]

According to the World Bank, in 2007 per capita income in the United States was more than 5 times greater than in Mexico—$46,040 compared with $8,340. Countries south of Mexico have even lower incomes, including El Salvador ($2,850) and Guatemala ($2,440). Many scholars insist that as long as such poverty persists in Mexico and Central American nations, no border controls or other efforts are going to keep people from crossing the U.S.-Mexico border in search of work. Therefore, they argue, resolving the issue of illegal immigration will require cooperating with the Mexican and other governments to establish treaties and programs that stimulate economic growth and wealth below the border. "Immigration, by definition, is a phenomenon of both sides of a frontier," notes Jeff Faux, a distinguished fellow at the Economic Policy Institute, a public policy research organization. Yet, he adds, "our egocentric

"An amnesty might be conceivable: but only after it was clear that it would not act as an invitation to further border crossings."[65]

— Ramesh Ponnuru, senior editor for the *National Review*.

American politics defines the question as if it can be entirely answered within our borders by unilateral government decisions. . . . Sooner or later, the U.S. will have to include Mexico in any serious effort to control illegal immigration."[68]

FACTS

- Article 1, Section 8 of the U.S. Constitution grants Congress the power "to establish an uniform Rule of Naturalization." This clause has been interpreted to grant control of immigration to Congress.
- On any given day U.S. Customs and Border Protection deploys 10,029 vehicles, 267 aircraft, 175 watercraft, and 188 equestrian patrols.
- According to a January 2009 Rasmussen poll, 60 percent of Americans believe the government should continue to build a fence along the U.S.-Mexico border, and 58 percent believe the U.S. military should be deployed along the border.
- U.S. Immigration and Customs Enforcement estimates that it would cost about $94 billion to deport the approximately 11 million illegal immigrants living in the United States.
- In a December 2008 Zogby poll, 52 percent of Americans opposed a new path to citizenship for illegal immigrants in the United States. However, 67 percent supported a path to citizenship for illegal immigrants if they pay taxes, pay a penalty, and learn English.
- According to a 2007 NBC/*Wall Street Journal* poll, 85 percent of Americans believe that deporting all illegal immigrants is not a realistic or achievable goal.

Related Organizations

American Immigration Law Foundation (AILF)

1331 G St. NW, Suite 200
Washington, DC 20005
phone: (202) 507-7500
fax: (202) 742-5619
e-mail: info@ailf.org
Web site: www.ailf.org

The AILF is a nonprofit educational and charitable organization that works to increase the public's understanding of immigration law and policy as well as the value of immigration to American society. It operates several programs, including its Legal Action Center, Curriculum Center, and Immigration Policy Center (IPC), a think tank that does research and analysis on issues related to immigration. The IPC publishes the monthly *Immigration Policy Focus* as well as various policy briefs, special reports, and fact sheets on immigration topics.

Center for Immigration Studies (CIS)

1522 K St. NW, Suite 820
Washington, DC 20005-1202
phone: (202) 466-8185
fax: (202) 466-8076
e-mail: center@cis.org
Web site: www.cis.org

The CIS is a nonprofit public policy research organization dedicated to analyzing the economic, social, demographic, and other impacts of immigration on the United States. The center advocates reduced legal immigration and strong enforcement of laws to prevent illegal immigration. It publishes numerous op-eds, such as "No Amnesty—Now or in Two Years," and policy reports, including *Homeward Bound: Recent Immigration Enforcement and the Decline in the Illegal Alien Population.*

Essential Worker Immigration Coalition (EWIC)

1615 H St. NW
Washington, DC 20062
phone: (202) 463-5931
fax: (202) 463-5931
e-mail: ewic@uschamber.com
Web site: www.ewic.org

The EWIC is a coalition of businesses, trade associations, and other organizations concerned with the shortage of both lesser-skilled and unskilled ("essential worker") labor. The coalition supports reform of immigration policies to make it easier to for U.S. companies to employ foreign workers. The EWIC publishes several reports on illegal immigration, including *The Economic Logic of Illegal Immigration* and *Dollars Without Sense: Underestimating the Value of Less-Educated Workers.*

Federation for American Immigration Reform (FAIR)

25 Massachusetts Ave. NW, Suite 300
Washington, DC 20001
phone: (202) 328-7004
fax: (202) 387-3447
Web site: www.fairus.org

FAIR is a nonprofit membership organization of concerned citizens dedicated to reforming the nation's immigration policies. FAIR seeks to improve border security, stop illegal immigration, and reduce legal immigration to about 300,000 persons per year. Its Web site offers numerous fact sheets and statistics, as well as the *Immigration Report* newsletter and reports such as *Illegal Immigrants and Crime Incidence* and *Immigration and National Security.*

Mexican American Legal Defense and Education Fund (MALDEF)

634 S. Spring St.
Los Angeles, CA 90014
phone: (213) 629-2512
Web site: www.maldef.org

MALDEF is a nonprofit organization that provides litigation, advocacy, and outreach in order to foster laws and programs to protect the civil rights of Latinos living in the United States, including those of illegal immigrants. Its Web site contains a section on immigration that outlines the efforts and successes of the group's immigrants' rights program and lists various publications on the immigration issue.

Migration Policy Institute (MPI)

1400 Sixteenth St. NW, Suite 300
Washington, DC 20036
phone: (202) 266-1940
fax: (202) 266-1900
Web site: www.migrationpolicy.org

The MPI is a nonprofit research organization that provides analysis, development, and evaluation of migration and refugee policies at the local, national, and international levels. Its work is guided by the belief that immigration is beneficial to society and that fair, smart immigration policies can promote social cohesion, economic vitality, and national security. The MPI publishes many fact sheets and reports, such as *Unauthorized Migrants: Numbers and Characteristics* and *US Border Enforcement: From Horseback to High-Tech.*

National Council of La Raza

1126 Sixteenth St. NW
Washington, DC 20036
phone: (202) 785-1670
fax: (202) 776-1792
e-mail: comments@nclr.org
Web site: www.nclr.org

The NCLR is the largest national Hispanic civil rights and advocacy organization in the United States. It works to improve opportunities for Hispanic Americans through research, policy analysis, and advocacy in five key areas: assets/investments, civil rights/immigration, education, employment and economic status, and health. It publishes fact sheets, position papers, and policy recommendations on immigration, including "Five Facts About Undocumented Workers in the United States."

National Immigration Forum

50 F St. NW, Suite 300
Washington, DC 20001
phone: (202) 347-0040
fax: (202) 347-0058
Web site: www.immigrationforum.org

The National Immigration Forum is an immigrant advocacy organization that promotes the view that immigrants are valuable to America and that newcomers should be welcomed and treated fairly. It seeks to increase cooperation and informed opinions on immigration issues in order to achieve immigration policy reform in accordance with its vision. Its Web site makes available various reports on immigration, including *Rethinking Crime and Immigration* and *Border Insecurity: U.S. Border-Enforcement Policies and National Security.*

NumbersUSA

1601 N. Kent St., Suite 1100
Arlington, VA 22209
phone: (877) 885-7733
Web site: www.numbersusa.org

NumbersUSA is a nonprofit education and research organization that advocates for reduced immigration. It conducts studies on the impacts of high levels of immigration and educates the public, opinion leaders, and policy makers on the results of those and other studies. Its Web site offers articles, poll data, and statistical information in support of its views regarding the negative impact of immigration on the environment, the economy, and the job market.

Pew Hispanic Center

1615 L St. NW, Suite 700
Washington, DC 20036-5610
phone: (202) 419-3600
fax: (202) 419-3608
e-mail: info@pewhispanic.org
Web site: http://pewhispanic.org

The Pew Hispanic Center is a nonpartisan research organization that seeks to improve understanding of the role and influence of the U.S. Hispanic population. The center conducts and commissions studies and public opinion surveys on a wide range of topics, including immigration. Titles of relevant reports include *Trends in Unauthorized Immigration: Undocumented Inflow Now Trails Legal Inflow* and *A Rising Share: Hispanics and Federal Crime.*

Urban Institute

2100 M St. NW
Washington, DC 20037
phone: (202) 833-7200
Web site: www.urban.org

The Urban Institute gathers data, conducts research, evaluates programs, offers technical assistance, and educates Americans on social and economic issues in an effort to foster sound public policy and effective government. It publishes op-eds and reports on immigration, including the effect of immigration on African Americans. Titles of its immigration-related publications include *The Effects of Immigration on the Employment Outcomes of Black Americans* and *Immigration and Economic Mobility.*

U.S. Department of Homeland Security (DHS)

Washington, DC 20528
phone: (202) 282-8000
Web site: www.dhs.gov

The U.S. Department of Homeland Security, created in 2003, is the department of the federal government responsible for protecting the nation against terrorist attacks and other foreign incursions on U.S. soil. Control of immigration falls within the DHS and is handled primarily by two agencies: Immigration and Customs Enforcement and Customs and Border Protection. The Web sites of all three agencies (www.dhs.gov, www.ice.gov, www.cbp.gov) contain a wealth of statistics and reports on immigration and the enforcement of immigration laws.

For Further Research

Books

Edward Alden, *The Closing of the American Border: Terrorism, Immigration, and Security Since 9/11.* New York: HarperCollins, 2008.

J.D. Hayworth, *Whatever It Takes: Illegal Immigration, Border Security, and the War on Terror.* Washington, DC: Regnery, 2006.

Mark Krikorian, *The New Case Against Immigration: Both Legal and Illegal.* New York: Sentinel, 2008.

Heather Mac Donald, Victor Davis Hanson, and Steven Malanga, *The Immigration Solution: A Better Plan than Today's.* Chicago: Ivan R. Dee, 2007.

Debra A. Miller, *Illegal Immigration.* San Diego: ReferencePoint Press, 2007.

Tony Payan, *The Three U.S.-Mexico Border Wars: Drugs, Immigration, and Homeland Security.* Westport, CT: Praeger, 2006.

Jason L. Riley, *Let Them In: The Case for Open Borders.* New York: Penguin, 2008.

Tom Tancredo, *In Mortal Danger: The Battle for America's Border and Security.* Nashville: Cumberland House, 2006.

Periodicals

America, "Immigration Reform," February 2, 2006.

Sam Antonio, "The North American Union Invasion," *New American,* October 15, 2007.

Richard Brookhiser, "Fear of Outsiders," *Time,* June 11, 2007.

BusinessWeek, "Econ 101 on Illegal Immigrants," April 7, 2006.

Linda Chavez, "The Realities of Immigration," *Commentary,* July/August 2006.

Ellis Cose, "American-Born, but Still 'Alien'?" *Newsweek,* March 19, 2007.

David DeCosse, "Can Citizenship Be Earned? Legal Remedies for Undocumented Immigrants," *America,* October 13, 2008.

Economist, "English Patients," June 7, 2008.

———, "Nowhere to Hide," July 7, 2007.

Larry Greenley, "How to Fix Illegal Immigration," *New American,* March 3, 2008.

Patricia Kilday Hart, "Why Juan Can't Read," *Texas Monthly,* October 2006.

Patricia Hatch and Katherine Fennelly, "Unauthorized Immigrants: The Case for Earned Legalization," *National Voter,* June 2008.

Llewellyn D. Howell, "Ironies of Illegal Immigration," *USA Today,* July 2006.

Gary Jason, "Good for the Economy: Immigrants Are a Net Plus for America's Bottom Line," *Los Angeles Daily News,* January 14, 2007.

R. Cort Kirkwood, "Roadkillers," *New American,* April 2, 2007.

Mark Krikorian, "Enforcement Works," *Los Angeles Times,* September 2007.

Angie C. Marek, "The Immigration Minuet," *U.S. News & World Report,* July 24, 2006.

Doris Meissner, "Learning from History," *American Prospect,* November 2005.

New York Times, "The Great Immigration Panic," June 3, 2008.

John O'Sullivan, "But Shall It Prevail?" *National Review,* September 29, 2008.

Tim Padgett, "Home Work," *Time,* March 26, 2007.

Eyal Press, "Do Immigrants Make Us Safer?" *New York Times Magazine,* December 3, 2006.

Robert J. Sampson, "Open Doors Don't Invite Criminals," *New York Times,* March 11, 2006.

Bret Schulte, "In a New Country, Struggling to Fit In," *U.S. News & World Report,* May 26, 2008.

Jennifer Steinhauer, "Immigration and Gang Violence Propel Crusade," *New York Times,* May 15, 2008.

James Thayer, "The War on Snakeheads," *Weekly Standard,* April 19, 2006.

Nathan Thornburgh, "How Not to Treat the Guests," *Time,* June 4, 2007.

Jacob Vigdor, "Choices to Make on Immigration Policy," *Boston Globe,* May 19, 2008.

Washington Times, "Crime, Illegals and the Job Magnet," September 15, 2008.

Matt Welch, "Illegal Editor: Immigration Restrictions Hurt Legal Residents," *Reason,* October 2008.

Web Sites

Cato.org (www.cato.org). The Web site of the Cato Institute, a libertarian think tank, this site publishes articles and report from a libertarian point of view. Libertarians generally support open borders as part of their philosophy of free markets and individual liberty.

Human Events.com (humanevents.com). This Web site of the ultraconservative *Human Events* newspaper often presents articles on illegal immigration and immigration policy.

National Review Online (www.nationalreview.com). The Web site of the *National Review,* a weekly journal, this site frequently posts articles on immigration and immigration policy from a conservative viewpoint.

ProEnglish (www.proenglish.org). This site advocates making English the official language at all levels of government.

Reason Online (www.reason.com). The Web site of *Reason,* a weekly magazine published by the Reason Foundation, this site publishes many articles on immigration from the libertarian perspective.

Source Notes

Introduction: A Nation of Immigrants—and Laws

1. Quoted in *Time,* "Postcard: Postville," June 16, 2008, p. 6.
2. Quoted in Nigel Duara, William Petroski, and Grant Schulte, "Claims of ID Fraud Lead to Largest Raid in State History," *Des Moines (IA) Register,* May 12, 2008. www. desmoines register. com.
3 Quoted in U.S. Immigration and Customs Enforcement, "297 Convicted and Sentenced Following ICE Worksite Operation in Iowa," press release, May 23, 2008. www.ice.gov.
4 J.D. Hayworth, *Whatever It Takes: Illegal Immigration, Border Security, and the War on Terror.* Washington, DC: Regnery, p. 5.
5 Barack Obama, "Remarks to the National Council of La Raza," July 22, 2007. www.barackobama.com.

Chapter One: What Are the Origins of the Illegal Immigration Controversy?

6 Claire Lui, "How Illegal Immigration Was Born," *American Heritage,* May 7, 2007. www.americanheritage.com.
7 Tony Payan, *The Three U.S.-Mexico Border Wars: Drugs, Immigration, and Homeland Security.* Westport, CT: Praeger, 2006, p. 8.
8 Payan, *The Three U.S.-Mexico Border Wars,* p. 7.
9. David M. Reimers, "Immigration," *World Book Online Reference Center.* www.worldbookonline.com.
10. Payan, *The Three U.S.-Mexico Border Wars,* p. 10.
11. Payan, *The Three U.S.-Mexico Border Wars,* p. 11.
12. Katherine Fennelly, "U.S. Immigration: A Historical Perspective," *National Voter,* February 2007, p. 4.

13. Anthony York, "R.I.P. Prop. 187," *Salon,* July 30, 1999. www.salon.com.

Chapter Two: Does Illegal Immigration Harm the American Economy?

14. Ramesh Ponnuru, "Illegal Detour: Thinking Reasonably About Immigration," *National Review*, March 27, 2006, p. 24.

15. Mario Vargas Llosa, "The Fence of Lies," *New Statesman,* November 2, 2006, p. 36.

16. David Card, "Is the New Immigration Really So Bad?" Department of Economics, University of California, Berkeley, January 2005. www.phil.frb.org.

17. Llewellyn D. Howell, "Ironies of Illegal Immigration," *USA Today,* July 2006, p. 19.

18. Steven A. Camarota, "Immigration Is Hurting the U.S. Worker: Low Paid American Workers Have Borne the Heaviest Impact of Immigration," *Americas Quarterly,* Spring 2007. www.cis.org.

19. Thomas R. Eddlem, "Myth vs. Fact," *New American,* May 1, 2006, p. 23.

20. Quoted in Mark Krikorian, "Enforcement Works; Crackdowns on Illegal Immigrants Have Opened Up Jobs for Americans," *Los Angeles Times,* September 24, 2007, p. A15.

21. Quoted in David Liss, "Determining the Costs of Undocumented Immigrants to the U.S.," *LatinoLeaders,* October 2006, p. 46.

22. Steven A. Camarota, "The High Cost of Cheap Labor: Illegal Immigration and the Federal Budget," August 2004. www.cis.org.

23. Jack Martin and Ira Mehlman, "The Costs of Illegal Immigration to Californians," Federation for American Immigration Reform, November 2004. www.fairus.org.

24. Quoted in Rand Corporation, "Rand Study Shows Relatively Little Public Money Spent Providing Health Care to

Undocumented Immigrants," press release, November 14, 2006. www.rand.org.

25. Quoted in Rand Corporation, "Rand Study Shows Relatively Little Public Money Spent Providing Health Care to Undocumented Immigrants."

26. Ernesto Zedillo, "Migronomics Instead of Walls," *Forbes,* January 8, 2007, p. 25.

Chapter Three: Does Illegal Immigration Harm American Culture?

27. Quoted in CNN.com, "Rallies Across U.S. Call for Illegal Immigrant Rights," April 10, 2006. www.cnn.com.

28. Dan Stein, "Millions of Illegal Aliens Take to the Streets Demanding 'Rights' and Amnesty While the Government Refuses to Act," Federation for American Immigration Reform, May 2006. www.fairus.org.

29. Hayworth, *Whatever It Takes,* pp. 50–51.

30. Jacob L. Vigdor, "Measuring Immigrant Assimilation in the United States," Civic Report, Manhattan Institute for Policy Research, May 2008. www.manhattan-institute.org.

31. Mortimer B. Zuckerman, "A Little Sanity, Please," *U.S. News & World Report,* April 17, 2006, p. 74.

32. Jay Nordlinger, "Bassackwards: Construction Spanish and Other Signs of the Times," *National Review,* January 29, 2007, p. 30.

33. Shirin Hakimzadeh and D'Vera Cohn, "English Usage Among Hispanics in the United States," Pew Hispanic Center, November 29, 2007, p. i. http://pewhispanic.org.

34. Norman Gold, "Successful Bilingual Schools: Six Effective Programs in California," San Diego County Office of Education. www.bilingualeducation.org.

35. Thomas B. Parrish et al., *Effects of the Implementation of Proposition 227 on the Education of English Learners, K–12: Findings*

from a Five-Year Evaluation, American Institutes for Research and WestEd, January 24, 2006. www.air.org.

36. ProEnglish, "Why Official English?" www.proenglish.org.
37. Charles Krauthammer, "Let's Make It Official," *Time,* June 12, 2006, p. 112.
38. Walter A. Ewing, "Opportunity and Exclusion: A Brief History of U.S. Immigration Policy," Immigration Policy Center, November 25, 2008. www.immigrationpolicy.org.

Chapter Four: Does Illegal Immigration Lead to Increased Crime and Terrorism?

39. Federation for American Immigration Reform, "Illegal Immigrants and Crime Incidence," March 2007. www.fairus.org.
40. R. Cort Kirkwood, "Crime Wave," *New American,* January 8, 2007, p. 18.
41. Rubén G. Rumbaut and Walter A. Ewing, "The Myth of Immigrant Criminality and the Paradox of Assimilation: Incarceration Rates Among Native and Foreign-Born Men," Immigration Policy Center, Spring 2007, p.1.
42. Robert J. Sampson, "Rethinking Crime and Immigration," *Contexts,* Winter 2008, p. 29.
43. Robert F. Mulligan, "Do Immigrants Make Us Safer?" letter, *New York Times Magazine,* December 17, 2006. http://paws.wcu.edu.
44. Jessica M. Vaughan and Jon D. Feere, "Taking Back the Streets: ICE and Local Law Enforcement Target Immigrant Gangs," backgrounder, Center for Immigration Studies, October 2008. www.cis.org.
45. Vaughan and Feere, "Taking Back the Streets."
46. Vaughan and Feere, "Taking Back the Streets."
47. Quoted in Manhattan Institute for Policy Research, "Testimony: Immigration and the Alien Gang Epidemic: Problems and Solutions," April 13, 2005. www.manhattan-institute.org.
48. Jack Martin, "Immigration and National Security: A Checklist of Unfinished Reforms," Federation for American Immigration Reform, September 2008. www.fairus.org.

49. General Accountability Office, "Despite Progress, Weaknesses in Traveler Inspections Exist at Our Nation's Ports of Entry," January 3, 2008. www.gao.gov.

50. Majority Staff of the House Committee on Homeland Security Subcommittee on Investigations, "A Line in the Sand: Confronting the Threat at the Southwest Border," U.S. Representative Michael McCaul. www.house.gov.

51. Bennie G. Thompson, Bob Ethridge, and Sheila Jackson, "Partisan Report Distorts Real Problem at the Border," press release, October 20, 2006. http://homeland.house.gov.

52. Payan, *The Three U.S.-Mexico Border Wars,* p. 93.

53. Quoted in Alex Kingsbury, "Post-9/11 Antiterrorism Measures Should Be More Targeted, Says New Book," *U.S. News & World Report,* September 17, 2008. www.usnews.com.

54. Martin, "Immigration and National Security."

Chapter Five: How Should the Government Respond to Illegal Immigration?

55. Quoted in *American City & County,* "Border Town Fights Federal Fencing Plans," Gale Academic OneFile, March 1, 2008.

56. Payan, *The Three U.S.-Mexico Border Wars,* p. 120.

57. Quoted in "Federal Jury Finds South Dakota Couple Guilty of Abusing Their Workers," U.S. Immigration and Customs Enforcement press release, November 8, 2007. www.ice.gov.

58. Michael Chertoff, "Remarks at a Briefing on Immigration Enforcement and Border Security Efforts," Department of Homeland Security, February 22, 2008. www.dhs.gov.

59. National Council of La Raza and Urban Institute, *Paying the Price: The Impact of Immigration Raids on America's Children.* Washington, DC: National Council of La Raza, 2007, p. 4.

60. *Economist,* "A Haven Indeed," August 24, 2007, p. 29.

61. George F. Will, "Guard the Borders—and Face Facts, Too," *Washington Post,* March 30, 2006, p. A23.

62. Barack Obama, "Full Text of President Obama's Costa Mesa Town Hall Meeting," *Los Angeles Times,* March 18, 2009. http://latimesblogs.latimes.com.

63. Mark Krikorian, *The New Case Against Immigration: Both Legal and Illegal.* Washington, DC: Sentinel, 2008, p. 217.

64. Krikorian, *The New Case Against Immigration,* p. 216.

65. Ramesh Ponnuru, "The Home Front: What to Do About Domestic Policy," *National Review*, February 12, 2007, p. 17.

66. Thomas Wenski, "Hitting a Wall on Immigration," *Washington Post,* October 20, 2008, p. A15.

67. Joan B. Anderson and James Gerber, *Fifty Years of Change on the U.S.-Mexico Border: Growth, Development, and Quality of Life.* Austin: University of Texas Press, 2008, p. 139.

68. Jeff Faux, "What to Really Do About Immigration," *American Prospect,* January/February 2008, p. 41.

Index

About the Author

Scott Barbour received a bachelor's degree in English and a master's degree in social work from San Diego State University. He has written and edited numerous books on social issues, historical topics, and current events.